Black
in a
White
World

Black in a White World

An Incredible Couple Who Changed Lives

Constance Wheat Batty

Constance Wheat Batty, Ed.D.

BLACK IN A WHITE WORLD
AN INCREDIBLE COUPLE WHO CHANGED LIVES

All photos courtesy of Constance Batty except where otherwise noted:
New York Public Library (NYPL): Public domain, permission not required from for any uses: Queensboro Bridge, 59th Street, 1918 (NYPL); Harlem Tenement in Summer (NYPL), c. 1935, (NYPL); Pushcart vendors 8th Avenue at West 145th Street, Harlem, 5/8/39, (NYPL) Wikipedia: Map of Spain (public domain)

Cover photo: Use with permission from Constance Batty; Sculpture owned by Constance Batty. Vintage Tree of Life (Makonde?), 12" oval base, ebony, by Simau, Africa, c. 1955.

Cover and Book Design: IUniverse and J.A. Hopkins
Editing: Muriel Gold and J.A. Hopkins

iUniverse books may be ordered through booksellers or by contacting:

iUniverse
1663 Liberty Drive
Bloomington, IN 47403
www.iuniverse.com
844-349-9409

ISBN: 978-1-6632-2340-1 (sc)
ISBN: 978-1-6632-2341-8 (e)

Print information available on the last page.

DrBatty8@aol.com

iUniverse rev. date: 07/12/2021

Despite constant and subtle racism, this self-made
Black family became financially and socially successful
contributing members of their worldwide community.
Donald Lewis and Irma Lucille Wheat
1914-2010

The Family of Donald and Irma Wheat

Contents

Chapter Five

Chapter Six

Chapter Seven

Table of Figures

Dedication

This book is dedicated in loving memory
of my extraordinary parents,
Donald Louis and Irma Lucille Walker Wheat
who faithfully supported me through 77 years of life
and who remain in my everyday memories.
And to my beautiful daughters,
Judith N. Batty, Esq. and Alicia J. Batty Batts, Esq.
who conferred and shared many memories.

Acknowledgements

I wish to express my gratitude to the many people who saw me through the writing of this book; to all those who provided support, talked things over, read, wrote, offered comments, and assisted in the editing, proofreading and design.

Above all I want to thank my daughters, Judith Batty and Alicia Batts, who supported, encouraged and sometimes lectured me as I sent them drafts for input.

Many thanks to my editors and organizers supreme, Dr. Muriel Gold, C.M., and Janet A. Hopkins, M.A., who were devoted to creating the finished product. Copy editor Barbara Schuderer of Prescott, Arizona, provided additional editorial support and proofing. I deeply appreciate the early guidance and assistance of Kharmasis@hoverflymedia.com.

Thanks to my Point Brittany readers, Sheila Green, Laura Scattergood, Barbara Dalton and Cindy Tholkes. You participated in group readings and critiquing many chapters and are marvelous neighbors.

And finally, thanks to Beverly Adkins, Lavern Friedel and Patricia Patton who raised my courage, determination and stamina to write, and to the members of the Point Brittany Writers Workshop whose interest and motivation kept me writing.

Preface

Both my parents were born in 1914 and lived into the beginning of the 21st century. Life for the average citizen of the United States of America at the beginning of the 20th century was unlike our lives at the end of the century.

"Bricklayers earned 75 cents per hour; carpenters averaged 65 cents per hour. Many farmer laborers were paid $21.00 per month which included room and board. Women could not vote, and most were unemployed. Those who did work were usually paid considerably less than men performing similar tasks. The average life expectancy for men was 52 years and 56.8 years for women. Workers in factories were earning an average of $5.00 per day. The Bureau of Internal Revenue issued the first tax form: individuals paid a 1% tax on income over $3,000.00.

"The Panama Canal opened after 34 years of building. The world's first commercial airline flight was between St. Petersburg and Tampa and lasted 23 minutes. Greyhound Bus Lines began serving riders on May 21, and transportation was altered forever. In August, the first traffic light was installed in Cleveland, Ohio. The Model T Ford was selling for $440.00.

"Eggs were 35 cents a dozen; milk approximately 36 cents per gallon and a house could be purchased for $6,000.00. Most homes did not have indoor plumbing, and as late as 1940, only 55% of homes had complete indoor plumbing. Today we Americans consider bathtubs, cars, radios, smart phones and television sets to be important components of life.

"In 1914, about 60% of all children were enrolled in school, while only 13% of students earned a high school diploma. Less than 3% earned a bachelor's degree in college." (Melissa, 2014)

In July of 1910, a black boxer named Jack Johnson successfully defended his heavyweight title against Jim J. Jeffries, a white former undefeated heavyweight champion. Race riots erupted and at least 20 people were killed. (Britannica, 2018) There was an outcry around the country to ban the film of the fight. In 1912, Congress responded by passing a law which banned the distribution of prize fight films across state lines that remained valid for years. Many believed that films showing a black man winning a match would incite race riots.

African Americans experienced a life experience unlike those of most white Americans. Jim Crow Laws, lynching, segregation, oppression, discrimination, underpayment for same jobs, unemployment, prison, whites-only bathrooms or no bathrooms at all for people of color describe only a few of the issues faced by black Americans. In addition, no service was available to African Americans in hotels, restaurants, hospitals and even tax-supported public places.

Segregation and discrimination were the rule when Donald and Irma were born in a segregated New York hospital. These forces dominated their lives in both overt and subtle ways. Firemen and policemen in New York City were required to pass a written and oral exam. Minority candidates were frequently failed for no apparent reason. My father and a few other black firemen, however, passed the exam and were subsequently hired.

Depending on their work shift, firemen ate meals and slept in the firehouse. Those firemen who objected to working with minority men would not speak to them and would break any dish used by the minority fireman and cut or "lose" bedding used by them. It was necessary for my father to muster inner strength to perform his job.

Irma spent her childhood with a loving family who resided on the top floor of a tenement building occupied by families of limited means. Donald grew up in a suburban area of New York City with his family supported by his father, a Pullman Porter. They fell in love and married in their late teens.

Together, Donald and Irma owned one of the few minority-owned businesses in Corona, Long Island. State and local police were frequent visitors and would ask aggressively what was "going on" in the back room, though they were consistently told it was a stockroom for the store. Sometimes if I worked at the store alone, I called my father to come to the store. Upon his arrival he would explain that he was a fireman and that he would never leave his daughter to manage a difficult situation.

Figure 1 Don Wheat (right), Engine 316, 27-12 Kearney St, East Elmhurst, New York

The sudden change in the attitudes of the policemen amazed me. The camaraderie amongst New York City Union and civil service members overrode the color issue.

When they owned Wheat's Wholesale Butter and Eggs, Donald and Irma's trucks traveled back and forth between lower Manhattan and their farm in Roxbury, New York. As he picked up eggs all over the state and delivered them in the city, state troopers frequently stopped my father. He ensured proper current licenses were available in the truck. Even after seeing the registration, officers would ask about the ownership of the vehicle. Interrogations about the origins of the eggs and other racially motivated questions were the norm.

In the early 1960s, soon after the death of their only son, my parents moved to Spain and did not return to the United States until 1978. After leaving the generally colorblind Spain and moving to St. Petersburg, Florida, Donald and Irma once again found themselves in a world where race was a major factor.

Few black delegates from Florida attended national conventions. After campaigning, and in some cases, infighting among local Democrats, my father and mother, both 82 years old, were elected to the first integrated Florida Delegation to the 1996 Chicago National Convention. William Clinton was nominated as the Democratic choice for President of the

United States, a remarkable and historic event. My parents were the first African American delegates from Florida.

In years past, African Americans in the South were not allowed to vote and were not involved with delegations for any political party. In 1948, the Mississippi Delegation and part of the Alabama Delegation withdrew from the Democratic Convention. They joined other Southern Democrats to form the State's Rights Party to maintain discrimination when choosing delegates.

In 1964, the Mississippi Delegation consisted solely of white delegates. African Americans could not vote in that state. In 1965, The United States instituted voting rights for all citizens. The new law enabled some African Americans to vote. Nevertheless, great resistance remained, some of which lingers even today.

It is a credit to my parents' will and determination that they not only survived but thrived in this oppressive environment. During a discussion with my parents, my mother proudly mentioned, "We have helped other people. We have been fortunate with our lives. We want to share with others."

We didn't plan our lives, but good things sort of happened.

Introduction

In 1998, while driving around St. Petersburg, Florida, my parents and I began to discuss the operation of my car phone and the different issues associated with their purchasing one for their own car. I explained to them what I knew about the various wireless models currently available and the meaning of some of the new terminology associated with them.

My mother, 84 years old, commented on how her personal world and the world at large had changed. Telephones were not a major part of her life as she was growing up. "In fact, everything is different," she said. "Few people I knew drove automobiles nor used the kind of kitchen appliances common today."

Fortunately, my mother meticulously maintained, over the last 30 years of her life, a diary of their experiences. In addition, I accessed a myriad of photographs, slides, films, letters, newspaper articles, videos, and various programs and bulletins documenting the events of their lives.

As preparation for writing this biography, I recorded remembrances and interviews with my parents. After each session, I was amazed at how much more I learned about them. My admiration, respect and awe of these two strong, wonderful black people grew.

This book is a chronicle of the lives and unique experiences of my parents, Irma Lucille Walker Wheat and Donald Louis Wheat. They were municipal and state employees, politicians, respected community activists, volunteers, artists, church leaders, bridge players, successful entrepreneurs, businesspeople and fun-loving travelers who lived abroad in different parts of the world for more than a decade.

They provided one another with strength and unconditional support. They facilitated a lifestyle for four generations of independent, successful black Americans, all of whom contributed to the betterment of their race. They were beloved by their families.

The book reflects my parents' personal views of the world as it changed around them – from childhood to adulthood to their lives as senior citizens. Equally important and interesting are their recollections of their roles and experiences as spouses, parents, grandparents, great-grandparents and as African Americans in the United States.

Constance Wheat Batty, Ph.D.

Chapter One

Clarence Joseph Wheat Sr., "Daddy Man": 1888-1961

Clarence Wheat Sr., my paternal grandfather, was born in Augusta, Georgia, on February 26, 1889.[1] His wife, Leila Davies Wheat, was born about 1890 in Florence, South Carolina. The couple married in 1906.

Clarence was employed as a Pullman Porter. He had been a printer in Augusta but found the New York printers unionized and racist; he could not be a printer in the state unless he was a paid member of the union. Fathers, their sons and grandsons often dominated these trade unions. This policy effectively prevented blacks from membership in trade unions. As a result, many well-educated black men became Pullman Porters during this period of racial segregation in America.

One of the early labor unions in the United States was founded by the Brotherhood of Sleeping Car Porters. The president, A. Phillip Randolph, became known nationally and the organization positively impacted the families of the Porters and the entire United States. It sponsored social events for family members and supplemented organizations formed at historically black colleges that were

Figure 2 Clarence "Daddy Man" and friend, Roxbury, c. 1955

[1] He was perhaps the son of Charles H. Wheat and Melinda (maiden name unknown), both of whom were born circa 1872 in South Carolina. In 1907, Melinda Wheat remarried Sam Oliver, a coachman, and they moved from Augusta to New York sometime after 1910 where they lived next door to Clarence and Leila Wheat.

developed because many America states blocked black admission to private or state colleges. The Brotherhood created an understanding, a national awareness and knowledge about the value of labor unions.

As a child, I remember the importance given to addressing black men as "Mister," not boy or uncle and not by the first name. I suspect this came about because in many situations the title "Mister" was not accorded to black men. When I married my husband, everyone called his father Mr. Batty. Friends, church members, handy men, even his wife called him Mr. Batty.

It was commonly known that Porters distinctly disliked the name "George," but riders generally use it when interacting with the Porters. Larry Tye, author of *Rising from The Rails: Pullman Porters and the Making of the Black Middle Class*, notes that George W. Dulany, who founded the Society for the Prevention of Calling Sleeping Car Porter "George" (SPCSCPG), wrote and circulated a letter that injected a bit of humor into the situation. [I found a copy of the letter in the personal papers of Clarence Wheat, my grandfather.] Tye informs the reader that letter gained responses from not only Pullman Porters but from world dignitaries, all named George. The moniker did not amuse the Pullman Porters. (Tye, 2005)

In 1926, the Society for the Prevention of Calling Sleeping Car Porters "George" SPCSCPG persuaded the Pullman Company to install small racks in each car, displaying a card with the given name of the Porter on duty. Of the 12,000 Porters and waiters then working for Pullman, only 362 turned out to be named George.

As a Pullman Porter, Clarence received a steady income often doubled by generous tips that enabled him to provide well for his wife and five children. However, the role of porter was frequently difficult and sometimes demeaning. He was expected to provide services to demanding clients while being treated as a servant, or in some instances, as a piece of furniture. Nonetheless, Pullman Porters served with a smile. Because of the demanding jobs the Porters held under difficult circumstances, their interest and support of the next generation contributed to the rise of the black middle class. Not only did they provide financially for their children, but they also stressed to them the importance of a fine education. As a result, many prominent black Americans are the children and grandchildren of Pullman Porters.

Despite difficult circumstances, the typical porter could often benefit from many important and wealthy clients. Those porters who paid attention kept abreast of financial and political events in the world around them. At times, a porter would be assigned to maintain and care for the needs of an important dignitary, frequent customers of the railroad.

It was not unusual for the dignitary and the porter to develop a special bond. Porters were even given suggestions about purchasing stocks and bonds. Some dignitaries would use their influence to assist the Porter's child, especially if the child faced discrimination in his or her career choice.

Another benefit of the job was the porter's access to many types of expensive delicacies. Clarence brought home caviar, smoked oyster, marinated herring, fancy imported sausages, bacon and choice cuts of meat. Moreover, he was a hunter and a fisherman. The family ate all kinds of wild

Figure 3 Donald, Clarence, Leila, Ralph, Irma and Connie, c. 1937

game which Leila became an expert in preparing.

Clarence was often away from his family for long periods of time, running on the Canada to New York line and sometimes between New York and Texas. His son Donald told me that he never remembered having a conversation with his father; yet as a grandfather, Clarence was most attentive to his grandchildren. For example, he took me on my first boat trip with a group of Pullman Porter families. We sailed up the Hudson River to somewhere in the Bear Mountains. As a child, I was always concerned about my weight. However, on that boat trip the other passengers complimented me on my size. They thought I was much healthier than the skinny girls in their families. Clarence was enormously proud of me and introduced me to everyone on the boat. My parents, Donald and Irma Wheat, were pleased and surprised at the reception I received, and I was elated!

Grandmother Leila was home most of the time. She was a financial wizard who managed the family's business operations. I heard from my Aunt Mae Elizabeth Wheat[2] that Leila's brother received a financial settlement from a major business establishment. This settlement may have provided the financial means for Leila and Clarence to purchase several homes in Corona.

Adjacent to their big home, they built one of the few six-story apartment buildings in the area. When they built and repaired their properties, they demanded the crews include black workers. On one occasion, I remember my grandmother walking several blocks from 104th Street in Corona to their 112th Street rental house to take care of the furnace.

Sometime around 1955, the couple went their separate ways. Because my grandmother lived across the street from my parents, I continued my relationship with her. She died in Corona, Queens, New York, on June 12, 1946. I did not see much of my grandfather after they separated; he may have remarried. Clarence died in Corona on October 28, 1961. They are both buried in the segregated Flushing Cemetery.

---

[2] Mae, a schoolteacher, remained single and lived most of her life in Augusta, Georgia. She died in 1997 in Leon County, Florida.

Chapter Two

Donald Louis Wheat: 1914-2004

My name is Donald Louis Wheat. I was born on January 20, 1914, into a family of eventually five brothers and two sisters. Although the family lived in a rural area of Long Island called Corona,[3] I was born in Harlem Hospital in New York City, one of the few hospitals where African Americans received good medical care.

My parents, Clarence and Leila Davies Wheat, purchased a house in Corona and built one of the few multifamily houses in the area. Our house had gas lights; but by the late 1950s, these gas lights were just used as additional hooks for scarves, hats and umbrellas.

The Corona streets then looked quite different from the same streets today. Streetcars, ambulances and fire engines were pulled by horses. Ice men, calling out and selling ice to the housewives, were a common sight.

Public transportation was unavailable, and few owned cars. People in the neighborhood simply walked over the 59th Street Bridge into Manhattan, no small task. The bridge has been widened, repaired and now serves as a major artery to transport people to and from Manhattan. An arduous effort was made by me and others to ensure that public buses served the population of Corona during the evening hours.

---

[3] Corona is a small area on the north shore of Long Island which is geographically and politically part of New York City. Most of the houses are one or two-family houses with small back and front yards. The villages on Long Island were ethnic enclaves. Students were required to take buses to the nearby assigned high schools. Today, Corona is populated primarily by Hispanic people from various areas of the world.

Children made their own toys. Everyone owned an orange crate or some box with carriage or skate wheels attached, the preferred method of transportation for youngsters. We played stickball and hide and seek by the hour. Inside in the evening, we made up games, read and told spooky stories.

I don't recall having a radio for most of my childhood; however, we purchased the first player piano on the block. A roll of paper inserted into the piano directed the keys. We would pump the pedals and listen to all kinds of music while we dramatically pretended to play the keys.

Figure 4 Queensboro Bridge, 59th Street, 1918 (NYPL)

The families who lived in the Corona neighborhood during my childhood truly represented the world. I played with children who spoke different languages, including halting to perfect English. None of this was an issue.

Two German families were our immediate neighbors during World War I. Because the United States and Germany were on opposite sides, the German children were subjects of harassment. Their parents did not allow them to go many feet beyond their house. To play with them, we were told to stay near our houses.

I was in the primary grades at Public School 92 when my sister Voncille contracted polio. Upon the advice of her doctor, my family moved to the San Fernando Valley in California where I attended school from second to fifth grade. Tragically, she died in California and our family moved back to New York. We moved to St. Nicholas Place in Harlem as our house in Corona was under lease to another family.

Living in St. Nicholas Place – nicknamed Sugar Hill – was exciting and interesting, indeed. The area was home to many successful black people during a time of rampant housing discrimination and segregation. Local heroes, Harry Wills and Kid Chocolate, both black boxers, lived nearby. Jack Dempsey, the heavyweight champion of the world, refused to fight Wills because of his race, but to the people in the world around me, Wills was the champion. Wills retired from boxing in 1932 and ran a successful real estate business in Harlem.

Eventually our family relocated to our house in Corona where countless other blacks had recently moved. Many of the men were Pullman Porters like my father Clarence. This work meant a steady income.

Figure 5 Sugar Hill, Harlem, c. 1930 (NYPL)

Most of my mother Leila's friends were wives of Pullman Porters and visited one another for tea. I believe the main objective was chitchat (gossip). Finances were not discussed with children present, nor did there seem to be any money problems.

I enjoyed school and was a good student. I passed the entrance exam and gained admission to Stuyvesant High School, the premier high school in New York City, a school for gifted young men. At that time, the school was in downtown New York, quite a commute from Corona. Only a few black students were admitted to the school, some light-skinned blacks choose to pass as white. I graduated in the early 1930s.

During my high school years, I was lucky enough to meet Harry Stevens. Harry owned most of the food concessions at all the arenas and stadiums in New York. For events anywhere in New York, prospective workers would meet at a designated spot and Harry would hire those he needed.

Some of the workers would slack off on the job and others would hide or pilfer money. Harry considered me a good worker and always selected me. I could be assured of a job whenever I showed up. I saw all the major sporting events. The experience may

Figure 6 Irma and Donald (r.) with friends.

account for the fact that I am not enthusiastic about any sport. At any rate, I always had money of my own.

I became quite the young man about town. Mothers liked me. I was mannerly, well-spoken and considered handsome and smart. But alas, Dashing Don was short lived. I took Irma Lucille Walker to my senior prom, fell in love and married her. We have enjoyed a lifetime of marital bliss.

Chapter Three

Irma Lucille Walker Wheat: 1914-2010

My name is Irma Lucille Walker Wheat. I was born in Chicago, Illinois, to James Jefferson and Lucille "Tillie" Hawkins Walker on March 15, 1914.[4] I was the third child in a family of 11 children born to James and Lucille Hawkins Walker. Our family left Chicago when I was five or six years of age. I do not have any memories of Chicago, but I have definite memories of our next moves.

Figure 7 Irma Lucille Walker Wheat, c. 1931

First, we moved to Newport News, Virginia. I developed hepatitis and my parents were told by the doctor that we should leave the area for my health. We enjoyed a brief, but interesting and well-remembered stay on my Uncle Josh's[5] farm in Willow Grove, Pennsylvania. Unlike our home in Chicago, we had no electricity; we children arose with the rising sun to perform simple chores. Sunrise was dramatic in the country – waves of color filled the sky.

The house was lit with gas mantles, thin gauze bulbs shaped like light bulbs, only lit by adults with a match. We had a "modern" water pump by the kitchen sink whereas most of the families in the area used

---

[4] Lucille Hawkins, born July 14,1884, in New Orleans, was the daughter of Berry and Annette C. Henderson Hawkins. Berry was a porter for the Duckworth & Turner Co. in New Orleans and son of Augustus and Lucy A. Hawkins. (see page 100)

[5] Joshua Christopher Walker, born May 2, 1887 in Newellton, Louisiana.

outdoor water pumps. A large tank near the stove held hot water heated by the stove. An outhouse was situated in the backyard. A cold trip in the winter where we used crumpled newspaper as toilet tissue. Certainly different from the fancy bathrooms of today.

I watched pigs on the farm to learn exactly what they were fed. My father was astounded at the pails of slop the pigs eagerly ate; some of the slop had maggots on the top. He decided no one in his family would ever eat pork. The first time I tasted the meat was while visiting Donald, my husband-to-be.

The large smallpox vaccination on my arm was given by a physician in Willow Grove. In my youth, vaccinations were relatively new. The vaccination on my arm was larger than a fifty-cent piece, and for a long time it produced an odd, rather unpleasant odor. For years I never, ever wore any garment that did not cover it.

I remember our weekly visits to the park in Willow Grove when I was five or six years old. John Philip Sousa's military band provided a concert every Sunday evening, a wonderful event. Such music brings memories of my childhood. Today, the Willow Grove Park has been replaced by a large shopping center with a crowded parking lot.

Our family moved to wherever my father was employed. In 1922, when I was about eight years of age, he moved our family of seven children to Harlem, a section of New York City. We remained in Harlem for the duration of my childhood where three more children were born.

My father, James J. Walker, was a bricklayer, a specialist, constructing fireplaces, chimneys and other structures that required curving lines of bricks. This occupation was unusual for an African American man in those days. Few craft unions—or any unions—were open to African Americans. One had to be a union member to work.

The payment of his union dues came above all else. When quite young, my sister and I took the subway the eight miles to South Ferry to pay his union dues. On occasion, we would get lost, but no one was concerned because they knew we would eventually get home safely.

My relationship with my father was like the relationships my friends experienced with their fathers. He was the disciplinarian in the family. We all obeyed him without question. He reviewed our magazines and designated the articles he deemed appropriate for us to read. My sister and

I read only those articles. Today, I find it difficult to believe we were that obedient.

When he came home, he expected his wife to wait on him and his children to obey him. He was an avid sports fan and listened intently to all sports on the radio. This pastime, of course, required that all 11 children in the house be silent. Perhaps why few of my brothers and sisters were sports fans as adults.

Today, Harlem is internationally known as the Black Mecca of the world; but historically, Harlem has been home to Dutch, Irish, German, Italian and Jewish people. Originally settled by the Dutch in

Figure 10 Lucille "Tillie" Hawkins Walker c. 1940

1658, it was largely farmland and undeveloped territory for approximately 200 years. As New York's population grew, residential and commercial expansion moved northward to Harlem.

In 1904, a main subway line transported resident in and out of Harlem encouraging the development of multiple-family apartment buildings. Real estate agent and entrepreneur Philip Payton approached Harlem landlords, promising to fill the unoccupied properties with black tenants. Nationwide, blacks were denied housing as well as in large portions of New York City. Blacks poured into Harlem from lower Manhattan, the American South and the Caribbean, the largest migration of people within the United States.

Harlem is presently experiencing a new renaissance. Today, a brief walk through any section of the community will reveal the sights and sounds of construction crews at work developing properties. Tour buses bring tourists from around the world in record numbers to absorb the extraordinary multi-ethnic culture of The Black Capital of America.

In the 1930 Census the family was living in a tenement building on 8th Avenue.

In Harlem, we lived in tall tenement buildings and always on the top floor. Contrary to current rental practices, the higher floors, which required walking up flights of stairs, contained the most economical apartments for tenants.

The front door of each apartment opened into a long hallway. Beyond the door was a front parlor, while the bedrooms were on either side of the long hall. The large dining room and the kitchen were at the other end of the hall. Somewhere in the apartment was the room we referred to as the bathroom, but it was just a small room containing only a toilet. The porcelain bathtub was kept in the kitchen. Although we bathed regularly, a daily bath for each of 13 people was not feasible with only one tub!

Everyone I knew lived in just such an apartment. Our dining room was larger than most and accommodated all 13 of us for our daily six o'clock dinner. We were expected to be present and on time for dinner. Preceding dinner, we always sang grace as we held hands with each other

Figure 8 Harlem tenement in summer, c. 1935 (NYPL)

around the table. If on rare occasions one of us did not arrive home in time for dinner, my mother, unbeknownst to my father, would slip some food to the wayward child.

The Harlem of my childhood in the twenties was vastly different from the Harlem of today. My world felt safe to me. I had freedom to travel around my little piece of the universe. Locked doors were not the norm, nor was violence of any kind.

Apple stands filled the streets after the 1929 stock market crash. I was 15 years old and able to observe and understand more of the world around me. Unemployed men sold apples and other items from carts in the street. It was a simple way to earn a minimal income. Life changed for many families because of the crash. This period was the only time I remember my father not working.

How thrilled some of us were when we enrolled in a class taught by the only African American teacher in public school. In general, teachers were revered. Pupils speaking to any teacher in a rude manner was unheard of in my world. School was a wonderful place to be.

Trucks traveled up and down the streets all day. Mothers gave their soiled laundry to the wet wash truck driver and in a few days the driver returned with the laundry—wet, but clean. It was my job to separate the clothes from one another because the laundry was returned quite tangled.

We did not have a refrigerator, so we purchased blocks of ice every one or two days from the ice truck driver. The ice was placed into the icebox. The melting water traveled down a pipe into a large bucket. The bucket needed to be emptied once or twice a day.

My mother, Lucille Hawkins, or "Tillie" as she was called, was a quiet, calm person who was always home. In retrospect, I suspect she rarely went out of the apartment. She had very few friends. Her life revolved around my father and their 11 children. This was the norm for many wives and mothers in the world I lived in as a child.

Large pots on the stove contained our hearty "one dish" meals. My mother's ongoing concern was preparing enough dinner to fill the bottomless stomachs of my brothers. On Saturdays and Wednesdays, my mother baked bread. The wonderful aroma filled the apartment. Today, whenever I pass a bakery or smell bread baking, I think of my childhood days. However, even a child's life can look greener on the other side of the fence. When my cousins came to visit, they frequently brought store-bought bread, a great treat.

In addition to bread, my mother regularly made brown soap in a large pot on the stove. After the liquid soap cooled and hardened, my sister and I cut the soap into cakes used to wash the laundry.

My father, James, frequently worked out of town during the week, so occasionally my mother and I would enjoy going to a Friday afternoon movie. Another favorite time of mine was to rise early in the morning to sit and talk with Mother as we drank tea. I still drink tea today when I want to relax my mind and body.

Figure 9 Pushcart vendors 8th Avenue at West 145th Street, Harlem, 5/8/39 (NYPL)

No one I knew felt deprived or unhappy. Our lives were structured, and all the kids knew what was expected of them, not only in their own families, but in the families of their neighbors.

One neighbor, unbeknownst to her mother-in-law, did not adhere fully to the Jewish dietary laws. When the neighborhood children spotted the mother-in-law arriving for a visit, the children would dash upstairs to alert her of the impending visit. This news would activate a flurry of excitement. All inappropriate foods in her house were dispersed by the children to other residences. Thinking back about that now, I see both the seriousness and humor of the situation. This ritual demonstrated true multicultural understanding.

My siblings and I read many books, played jacks, hopscotch, and played stickball in the street by the hours. We "double-dutched" using two jump ropes turning at the same time; I can still jump double-dutch much to the surprise of my great grandchildren.

Some Saturdays, we went to the movies where we would spend the entire afternoon. We saw a double feature, cartoons, a serial movie like soap operas of today, and sometimes *The News of The Week*.

As many young ladies did, I took piano lessons while my brothers were reluctant violin students. We walked to our music teachers' homes. We paid the grand sum of 25 cents a lesson. Even now I can still play a mean scale or two.

Figure 10 Harlem Children playing in the street, 1929 (NYPL)

I brought home stacks of books from the public library. The joy of reading remained with me all my life. Zane Grey was among my favorite authors. I would sneak into the bathroom at night to read, a problem because we had only one bathroom for all 13 of us.

We children got along well together. The older siblings looked out for their younger brothers and sisters. Youngsters, not only from my family but from many other families, going on errands with small children in tow. I was responsible for two of my youngest brothers. I would playhouse with them, as did other girls on my block.

Each of us had chores and errands to complete. We had a system to enforce each other's good behavior. With so many siblings traveling in and around the house, privacy was unknown. If I dared violate any rules, whoever saw me (someone always did) would extract a favor as payment for silence. My mother must have wondered why all her lovely children frequently did one another's chores.

An exciting event during my childhood was the infrequent car ride. When a visitor would arrive in a car, the child in the family would convince the driver to take all of us for a ride. If the driver consented, neighborhood children would pile into the car for a ride around the block, a real treat. The child responsible for the ride would be a hero for the rest of the day.

I so appreciate the life I take pleasure in today. As a child, I could not have imagined my luck. Neither reading a crystal ball nor going to a fortune teller could have predicted the wonderful experiences I have enjoyed and continue to enjoy.

Chapter Four

Family Memories: Constance J. Wheat Batty

Donald L. and Irma Walker Wheat Marry: 1931

My parents, Donald and Irma Walker Wheat, met at the Savoy Ballroom in Harlem. The Savoy, an exciting place, was filled with young black people dancing and having fun. Irma fibbed, telling her mother she attended a tea at church and needed a few coins for the collection. Instead, she used these coins to jump on the subway and head to the Savoy. It is not clear whether Irma's mother ever discovered her Sunday afternoon whereabouts.

Figure 11 Irma, Connie and Donald Wheat, c. 1937

Donald and Irma married in 1931. They rented an apartment adjacent to Central Park, which gave the family access to the Central Park Zoo and to the playground. Much to their joy and the joy of their families, their first grandchild was born – me – Constance Wheat on February 25, 1933.

On May 24, 1934, my father joined the New York National Guard, Company 369th Infantry, and went to training at Camp Smith, located in Westchester County overlooking the Hudson River. The rugged mountains provided ideal terrain for the light infantry training.

My father passed the written and physical exams for the New York City Firemen. He could be spotted a block away in his uniform walking home; and I, wearing roller skates, would fly down the street and crash into him. Always reserved, he must have held some private thoughts about this heavy child crashing into him after he worked a full shift.

My parents were resourceful and served each other as a team. For each new business endeavor, Mother provided support for success. Her duties included all the paperwork: checks, mail, appointments, typing, and phone service.

Together, they sponsored big dances/ parties for the community and for their own profit. They would rent the main room of the nearby armory, hire a name band and sell tickets in our store and many other places. The event was marketed as "Dance with Don."

Figure 12 Donald (r.) at Camp Smith, c. 1934

Father and several friends also purchased houses in need of repair. The men would repair and replace everything in the building then put it on the market. The sale of one of these houses always prompted a small celebration in our store.

Wheat's Luncheonette: 1948

Late into the 1940s, few black people owned small businesses. Because my father grew up in Corona and his parents were owners of multiple properties in Corona, his family was well known and supported. Consequently, my parents decided to purchase a small store they named Wheat's Luncheonette on Northern Boulevard, the main street though many communities adjacent to Flushing Bay on the north shore of Long Island.

Our store was a well-stocked businessman's luncheonette and stationery store. We sold

Figure 13 Donald Louis Wheat, c. 1937

whatever a customer needed or wanted. If we did not have it, we found it. Patrons could buy lunches, hamburgers, ice cream and sodas at a long counter in the middle of the store. We sold newspapers and magazines from everywhere, including local newspapers and black newspapers from all over the country. I became an avid reader of all of them.

We carried cigars, cigarettes, tobacco, school supplies, toiletry articles for men and women, nonprescription medicines and candy, and it was one of the few local establishments where customers could purchase American Express money orders. To provide American Express services to the community, the owner was investigated before being bonded.

We even sold snuff, a chewing tobacco product bagged and saved under the counter for the customer who secretly requested it.

A glass-enclosed counter of penny candies enticed children. They would walk up and down in front of it and point to whatever special treat

Figure 14 Irma
Walker Wheat

they planned to purchase with their three or four pennies. My parents insisted that all staff and family must remain courteous to all customers.

One youngster spent quite a bit of time looking at the different candies and changing her decisions. "Maybe I will get this or maybe that," she said. Finally, my younger sister, Judith, explained in a strident voice, "I know what you can get – you can get out." I was shocked and tickled that she spoke to a customer in such a way. I am happy to have that small, pleasant memory of my sister. Ill for several years, she passed away from Hodgkin's disease in 1953 at the age of 13.

Many well-known celebrities made their homes in Corona. Some came into our store on a regular basis, including Louis Armstrong, a popular singer, saxophonist and bandleader. On Northern Boulevard near our store, a chicken barbeque restaurant was owned in the 1950s by Hollywood actor, Sidney Poitier. Poitier and calypso singer Harry Belafonte later became famous, but at this time, Sidney was just a regular guy who would drop into our store for a visit. Unfortunately, his restaurant eventually burned down. We often spotted Ella Fitzgerald walking around the neighborhood in her expensive mink coat. My aunt Ruth thought Ella, "looked like the devil" because she was so casually dressed underneath the coat.

Community Activism: 1941

The 1940s were trying years for Donald and Irma. The ethnic face of the United States was changing. Many black men in the newly desegregated army fought for the rights of others during Harry Truman's presidency. Upon arrival home, these soldiers demanded various rights and privileges common to other veterans.

Veterans who returned to New York City were given points on civil service exams. Because their jobs (policemen, firemen) were considered essential, non-veterans were not promoted and not allowed to join the military.

In 1940, my father was a founder of the Vulcan Society, a successful organization of African American firemen promoting equal opportunities for blacks. In 1944, the Vulcan Society forced a public hearing before the city council to expose some of the segregated practices. As a result, in 1946, a clause passed in the regulations banning racial practices in the fire department.

Donald is presenting the Award of Valor to Fireman Henry Whitfield in this 1947 photograph.[6] Donald organized many special occasions and dances to support their efforts and hired a Corona friend, Tito Puente[7], and

Figure 15 Award of Valor Presentation
(Don Wheat, far left).

---

[6] Figure 15 includes (front row from left to right): Donald L. Wheat; Lt. Lundroy White; Henry Whitfield (recipient); Commissioner Frank J. Quayle; President Robert O. Lowery, the first African American Fire Commissioner of New York City; and Chief Wesley A. Williams, the founder of the Vulcan Society and the grandson of an escaped slave who traveled the underground railroad to New York City.

[7] Tito Puente became a famous Puerto Rican-American musician, songwriter and record producer.

his band to play. Puente was so successful playing popular Afro-Cuban rhythms that many people mistakenly identified him as Cuban.

The civil rights movement blossomed and flourished. Job opportunities increased slowly. Protests, boycotts and marches were somewhat successful, even though these civil rights activities frequently accompanied violence. There was much joy when a young neighborhood woman was hired as the first minority salesperson at Macy's Department Store.

Despite my parents' busy schedules, they remained actively involved in the local chapter of both the National Association for the Advancement of Colored People (NAACP) and the Democratic Party of Corona. My mother was the recordkeeper for many of their programs and activities.

Donald and Irma employed several young people at the store to whom they frequently served as mentors. Many years later, they were in Washington D.C. waiting to enter a district court because their granddaughter Judith, named after my sister, was scheduled to present in an upcoming trial.

People in line, including my parents, were chatting and laughing when young man suddenly appeared, "I recognized you both by your laughs. You are the Wheats. You gave me my first job as a teenager, and I remember all the life lessons you both taught me. I am so happy to see you."

Passengers rode the New York City subway to Long Island City until midnight. No public transportation existed for commuters to reach the many small communities along Northern Boulevard, including Corona. My parents successfully petitioned the local transportation company to provide nighttime service into Corona.

The Death of My Sister, Judith Wheat: 1954

One evening in the early 1950s while my mother, Irma, washed my sister Judith's hair, she discovered a strange lump on Judith's neck. At the time Judith was about ten years old. After tests and visits to medical specialists, they gave her a diagnosis of Hodgkin's lymphoma.

Because of her illness, my parents decided to buy a house in an upscale Long Island community, Springfield Gardens. An eventful move. On moving day, the movers packed up our old refrigerator. Much to the surprise of all of us, the shoe I lost on the day of my high school graduation was there under the refrigerator. From then on, whenever anyone in the family lost something, the frequent question was "Did you check under the refrigerator?"

Our Corona neighbors were happy for us but concerned because my parents possessed the only television in the neighborhood. During one vacation from college, I was bemoaning the fact that my home friends claimed to have a wider and wilder social life in New York City than I had in upstate New York. After listening to my regret that I was attending a school in upstate New York, Mother said to me, "Connie, the girls have spent most evenings in our living room watching Ed Sullivan and Lucille Ball. I cannot imagine when all of this partying took place."

Our new house had a charming room on the first floor with wraparound windows and a lovely view. My father prepared it for Judith and equipped it with a hospital bed decorated as she liked. Friends could visit her when she felt up to it. Judith could walk with a companion through an adjacent large lot filled with trees and small animals.

Judith became progressively weaker until she was unable to attend school or to walk any distance. I was away at college, and on one weekend I invited Judith to visit me. She was provided a special first-class seat on the plane and other amenities that made her trip pleasant. We knew she was dying, and we tried to provide her with as much joy as possible.

Judith passed away on January 23, 1954, at only 13 years old. The minister at her funeral reminded us that Judith always had a smile on her face, and we could see her smile behind the clouds if we looked. Whenever I am in an airplane, I think about my sister as we fly above the clouds.

Many years after her death, my mother's sister told me of a conversation with Judith. "Mother and Connie think I am getting better, but I know I am going to die." I was shocked and deeply sorry. I realized we pretended around Judith and that left her to truly die alone.

During Judith's illness and subsequent death, my

Figure 16 Irma, Connie, Judith and Donald Wheat, c. 1949

21

parents endured a long daily drive to their store. This presented new challenges, and my mother began to complain of not feeling well and was tired much of the time. Mother consulted several physicians, and soon discovered she was pregnant. That was not wonderful news to my parents, though I was excited and pleased.

My brother, Donnie, was born in the fall of 1954, shortly before the family decided to spend the summer looking around upstate New York for a rural community. I was teaching at the time, and the school secretary was kind enough to call the hospital to inquire of Donnie's birth.

My Parents Move to Roxbury: 1955

When my father retired, my parents began planning a move to a rural area. After several years of searching, they purchased a 165-acre dairy farm in the Catskill Mountains on Hardscrabble Road in Roxbury, New York. They leased the land and dairy herd to a local farmer while my father focused on raising chickens.

Roxbury, primarily a farming community, provided quite a different lifestyle for my parents. During my many visits to Roxbury, I became acquainted with most of my parents' neighbors, hardworking second and third generation farmers remaining on the same nearby farms. Young teens drove the farm machines and rode their horses around town, and the local doctor made home visits. My infant brother, Donald Louis Wheat Jr., and my own children frequently required a visit from the friendly doctor.

Irma enrolled in extension courses for women. She learned to make leather bags and belts. I still use one of the leather wallets she made for me. They planted a large garden containing quite a variety of vegetables, fruits and berries. Mother learned to can fruits and freeze jellies, sauces and pie crusts. Daddy built shelves around the basement of this large house to store all the cans and jars. He prepared a large room to use as a freezer. All these activities demanded much of their time and expertise.

Judith and Alicia visited their grandparents often, learned how to collect eggs from the hen house, kill the chickens and make pies and jellies. Mother and Daddy purchased some cows that we all learned to milk. The cows impressed me and the comfort my children exhibited as they walked around the huge animals and assisted in milking them.

In addition to chores, there were many fun activities. We brought lunches, blankets and floats to the nearby creek. We quickly learned to ignore the thousands of mosquitoes that lived near the water. What glorious days!

Figure 17 Donald Wheat
on Roxbury Farm

Mother enjoyed the potluck church suppers that eventually turned into colossal banquets. One member repeatedly provided unadorned Jell-O as a contribution. The officers of the group finally passed a formal resolution banning Jell-O as the sole contribution. Such a series of events would happen only in a small community!

Wheat's Fresh Farm Eggs: 1957

In 1957, Donald developed a major business which he called "Wheat's Fresh Farm Butter and Eggs." As the number of eggs from their hens grew, he began delivering eggs to friends around New York. The egg crates quickly outgrew their car, so my parents purchased a truck. Father contracted with wholesale egg and butter dealers in Manhattan, the business part of New York City. Eventually, he obtained eggs from many farmers and became the only African American man licensed and bonded as a New York State butter and egg dealer. No other minority businessmen were involved in the wholesale egg business.

As my father's trucks traveled along New York State Highway, state troopers often stopped them. Some troopers were hostile while some welcomed a retired New York City fireman.

My father conducted all his business with checks, being bonded was valuable and not easily obtained, and meant that his checks were negotiable at the local farmers' banks. Mother, of course was the master bookkeeper.

My parents were actively involved in their church and with all their neighbors. In addition to my mother's garden, the farmer who leased their land provided farm produce.

Daddy never went alone to visit the farms because he was always concerned with his image as a black man. He did not want to provide any opportunity for false claims to be made against him. On many farms, the men were out working, which meant Donald usually dealt with the women of the family. Mother went with him in case a woman developed a notion to entertain my father.

On those occasions when I visited in Roxbury, I would accompany my dad on his rounds, an eyeopener for me. I saw farmers living in all kinds of conditions, from marvelous to extremely poor. I observed some farms where humans, chickens, dogs and cats all shared the same living quarters and dishes. Although the lifestyles differed from mine, everyone appeared healthy and happy.

Between 1950 and 1954, I attended a small state college in a rural part of New York State. Many of my classmates were the progeny of farmers; and because of my experiences, I was able to have meaningful conversations with them. Around tuition payment time, my classmates would contact their parents and request that a cow be sold.

Those were good years for our entire family. We enjoyed many visits from family members and friends. My parents took short shopping trips to Oneonta, Albany, Catskill Caves and annual county fairs.

Life was different when my children were little. Once or twice, I put Judith, my five-year-old daughter, on a nonstop bus from Buffalo to Oneonta to visit my parents in Roxbury. I pinned identification on her and her doll. The bus ran all night and the first stop in daytime was Oneonta.

Figure 18 Plucking chickens: Donald, Irma, friend, Lea-Ella Miles and unknown boy.

She and the bus driver were given written instructions: do not get off the bus at night, wait until daytime. All went well. Judith had a good night's sleep, and my parents were waiting for her when she arrived. I would not feel comfortable doing such a thing today.

Many of the farm children had horses to ride and care for. As their grandchildren grew, my parents purchased two horses for them. One black horse was named Midnight and the smaller horse who seemed docile was named Patience.

The Death of My Brother, Donald Wheat: 1961

My younger brother, in first grade at a local school, was a sweet child. His teachers told my mother he was exceptionally bright.

My cute brother died on December 29, 1961, in a tragic toboggan accident in the Roxbury mountains. He went sledding down a forbidden hill with an older visiting cousin. An automobile came along the generally unused road and hit both Donnie and our cousin. Donnie died instantly, and our cousin was injured. The family dog "King," a handsome boxer dog, stopped eating and pined away after Donnie perished.

Figure 19 Donnie Wheat, 1961

I lived in Buffalo by then and came home to a sad household. My distraught parents wanted to leave it all behind them. They had lost two children.

In 1966, they sold their business and left Roxbury for a few weeks in Europe to gather strength and regroup. The trip grew into two years of extensive travel around Europe and Africa. They fell in love with Spain and eventually moved there in 1969.

My Parents Move to Spain:1962

Many people create stereotypes or accept others' preconceived ideas about black people. The folks who believe blacks are unintelligent and lazy would not understand the unique insights and experiences my parents describe in writing about their travels. In their diaries, my parents refute these stereotypes with their descriptions and appreciation of the history and significance of what mankind has developed.

During the years they owned the store and the egg business, Mother and Daddy developed a positive relationship with immigrant shopkeepers. When they announced they were leaving the business for Europe, these Italian, French, Dutch and Austrian friends shared the names and addresses of their families in Europe who later welcomed my parents with open arms and provided them with marvelous adventures. When I joined them in travels around the globe, we saw few people of color, and never a black family of six traveling together.

It was not an easy move. My parents faced many decisions as they prepared to close their home and business and move from the United States, leaving behind family and friends. Friends both black and white often ask, "Why did your parents move to Spain?" Sometimes that question is asked by a person hiding feelings of shock and surprise.

Donald and Irma wanted a quiet place to grieve their two deceased children and to begin a new life for themselves. They lived on investments and a small New York City pension. Donald followed the ups and downs of the stock market and avidly read literature and periodicals pertaining to the market.

During the 1960s and 1970s, a great deal of unrest existed in the black communities of the United States. Sit-ins by active youngsters took place in public places such as restaurants, movies, libraries, schools, and public transportation where black people failed to gain admittance. Black people organized and demonstrated in various locales demanding voting rights, often accompanied by riots and police brutality.

The warmth of the climate and the Spanish people appealed to them after the years spent in the snowy mountains of the Catskills in New York State. In addition, the low cost of living proved advantageous.

Donald and Irma felt comfortable and welcome everywhere in Spain. People came from across the globe to visit or to live. These were the years of Franco, the Spanish dictator. A police presence ensured low crime rates, and inexpensive labor was readily available. Bikes were a major mode of transportation; anyone could ride a bike, leave it and retrieve it any time.

Altea, Spain: 1962

My parents found Altea, a small, quiet town in eastern Spain up in the mountains near Benidorm. They purchased a three-bedroom house overlooking the Mediterranean Sea, a short drive from the beach.

The Wheats entertained regularly on their expansive patio or in their large living room with a fireplace for cool winter evenings. The house overlooked the Mediterranean Sea. At night, we watched never-ending firework displays staged by nearby small towns celebrating various holidays.

The patio became Beauford's place, where my husband of 35 years could unwind with a glass of Spanish wine. Relaxation transformed Beauford. At home, he worked much of the time, as director of reading and federal funds for a Long Island school district. In addition, he served as adjunct reading instructor in the teacher education departments of Adelphi University, SUNY Old Westbury, and and taught at the New York University Reading Institute. He enjoyed playing the organ and directing the choir for church each Sunday. Moreover, he played at weddings, funerals and provided music for many other events. He was a busy man.

Daddy cultivated a large, lovely garden beside the house. Bountiful trees provided significant quantities of almonds for my parents and their neighbors. This abundance promoted discussions about delicious ways to serve these almonds. Mother was not as interested in the garden as her husband, but supportive nonetheless, and helped him design the landscaping. This garden required extensive

Figure 20 Our home in Altea, c. 1966

watering by hand each day because rain is scarce in Spain. A large water container was built under the house to hold purchased water.

Mother found a wonderful young woman to help around the house, and Donald employed helpers for various projects. When he installed window screens on the house, the neighborhood men came to watch and borrow tools. In a few months, all the nearby houses had screened windows.

Altea was an interesting community where people from all parts of the world lived and vacationed. Most people living on this quiet mountain were retired Dutch.

Figure 21 Map of Spain showing Altea

Shell Oil operated out of Indonesia and provided a luxurious lifestyle for their employees. When Japan invaded Indonesia, many of the Dutch Shell employees came to Spain and settled in Altea because its climate is similar to Indonesia.

Most of our Dutch neighbors spoke English, a required subject in their schools. Most radio and TV programs in Holland use English as the primary language, this worked well for our family. Coincidentally, the local bank president, a retired bank manager from New York, spoke English very well. My parents and the family of the bank president became great friends.

One summer, 12-year-old cousin Lea-Ella Miles, my father's sister Ruth's only child, spent the summer with us in Spain. She had broad interests and enjoyed the traveling and the exquisite dining with my parents and family. The closest neighbor had a pool, where the children were welcome to swim.

We were later happy she experienced a pleasing vacation before her untimely death. Lea-Ella was riding the school bus after a basketball game; she and other students leaned out of the window as the bus turned the corner. She was struck by a tree bough. Another family tragedy.

Checkpoint Charlie: 1967

A heat wave enveloped much of Europe, so our family left my parents' house in Spain and headed north. Donald and Irma Wheat were dedicated to extensive map reading and weather judging. We planned to drive to the Scandinavian parts of Europe in search of cooler weather.

All six of us, my parents, Beauford, and our two children, Judith and Alicia, piled into my parents' Volkswagen. Daddy drove the entire time and we finally ended up in Germany.

In 1967, tension existed between Russia and the rest of the world, especially between the United States and Russia. Germany was divided as spoils of the war and a concrete barrier, known as the Berlin Wall, separated West and East Berlin.

The main gate between East and West Berlin, known as "Checkpoint Charlie," consisted of a barbed wire fence surrounded by armed guards. Going from one side of Berlin to the other was complicated and not always successful. East Berliners invented a wide variety of methods to escape through Checkpoint Charlie.

On the day we visited Berlin, a young lady situated on the west side of the Wall began to slowly strip. The East Berlin soldiers, fascinated by her actions, stared happily as her boyfriend quietly slipped across the checkpoint to join her.

When our family arrived at the gate, my father ventured inside and eventually came out with entrance passes for us all. Later, we discovered that acquiring permission to venture into East Berlin was, indeed, very unusual. Frequently in Europe, a carload of black people proved to be advantageous, though questions regarding our origin, purpose and relationships to one another were expected. We found it difficult to convince the Europeans we were neither famous nor rich, but merely ordinary Americans traveling throughout Europe.

The occupants of our small car ranged from toddlers to grandparents. Daddy developed a positive rapport with most people. We knew if anyone could obtain permission to enter East Berlin, it would be Dad. Our pass entitled us to remain in East Berlin for a few hours and to catch a ferry to the Scandinavian Peninsula that evening.

The difference between East and West Berlin was remarkable. West Berlin had brightly lit streets and fancy store windows. Well-dressed people strolled the streets, gregarious and content. By contrast, East Berlin was gloomy. The few people we observed wore dark, simple clothing, each alone and noncommunicative.

Alas, the car developed a flat tire. Tourists were not allowed to spend western money in East Berlin, we could not purchase a tire or have the flat repaired. Suddenly three East Berliners appeared. With no conversation, smiles or exchanges, they opened the trunk, retrieved the spare, and replaced the flat tire. My dad attempted to thank them, but they simply walked away. The incident surprised us.

We missed the last ferry and returned to Checkpoint Charlie. It seems that *no one* returns to Checkpoint Charlie. We were immediately under suspicion. "Why did you return?" "Why did you puncture your tire?" "Who are you trying to sneak out of East Berlin?" "Who are the parents of the baby?" All questions were delivered by a young soldier who apparently had taken a few English lessons. Beauford who had served in the United States military in Germany, delivered a few words in German. Still, communication was limited, and the situation filled us with trepidation.

The soldiers removed and opened all our luggage, removed the car seats, searched the bottom of the car with a mirror at the end of a stick, and inspected the gas tank with another stick and mirror. This exercise took several hours and was the only time in my life I noticed my father nervous. His brow was wet, and he was uncharacteristically quiet. Seeing my father anxious dampened my spirits. My entire family was behind the Iron Curtain and no one in the whole world knew our whereabouts.

Eventually we were released. Relieved, my parents drove out of Germany and took us to the airport. My family took the next flight out of Germany for Spain.

Connie Shares a Special Day in England: 1979

Judith lived and worked in London near the world-famous Harrods, jokingly called her neighborhood store. While visiting her, we visited friends of my parents near Buxton. I smile when I think of the jazz concert our family later attended in this small town in northern England.

That morning was foggy and dark, the hilly terrain devoid of traffic. Most of the occupants in our car were half asleep. We spent the night in one of the many offbeat English castles converted into hotels.

I glanced out the window and exclaimed, "Look, there's a tiger!" No one responded. The tiger passed from view, and I began to wonder about my sanity. Was I hallucinating? Why would a tiger be standing on the moors of England?

All was quiet in the car. Why did I open my mouth? Why did I blurt out such a statement? Fortunately, we soon passed a large bulletin board: Royal Conservatory for Animals. I was quite relieved and more confident in my sanity.

We arrived at the home of friends my parents had met in Spain and discovered our hostess, Jane, was the mayoress of the small town near Buxton. She and her husband, Peter, treated us to a delicious English meal.

Jane was scheduled to attend a jazz performance by a band from Liverpool. She invited us to accompany her. Judith, not interested in attending a concert featuring an unknown-to-her band from Liverpool, was of course polite. When we arrived at the auditorium, we were shown to special seats as guests of the local dignitary. Jane wore her full regalia, including a large medallion on a heavy gold chain. We could not slink to the back.

Much to our surprise, the band was fabulous. The five band members, professional men in various occupations and lifelong friends, gathered once a week for the past 45 years to play jazz. Feelings of joy and good times filled the small hall.

For some reason, the musicians believed my father, Donald, was a visiting musician. Here in a small town in northern England, they treated us as VIPs. One of the band members came over to shake Dad's hand, exclaiming to the attendees how proud they were to have a distinguished musician in the audience. We attempted to explain that my father was no one special, and certainly not a jazz musician.

Judith whispered, "Tell Grandmother and Granddaddy to sit and be quiet." Given the audience and my parents, I knew that was impossible. My dad waved to everyone, my mother nodded and smiled. It was easy to accept the accolades of the audience. We all settled in to enjoy the rest of the evening.

Chapter Five

Irma Walker Wheat: 1965-1976

Our European Tour: 1965[8]

After extensive preparations, deliberations, apprehensions and meditations, we climbed into our old faithful Chevy station wagon loaded with 11 pieces of assorted luggage. One last look at the old Roxbury homestead and off we went, bound for New York City to prepare for Tuesday's jet flight to Europe.

Upon arriving in New York, we drove to Kennedy Airport to verify our plane reservation. Due to the World's Fair, the hotels were booked. Luckily, we found a motel in nearby New Jersey.

The long-awaited day finally arrived. We were all set for our European Tour. While I visited a beauty parlor for a final treatment, Donald and a friend took care of checking in the baggage at the airport. Friends wined and dined us until we boarded the plane.

Our daughter, Connie, and her family joined us later. We all drove to the airport. Some of our friends came to wish us bon voyage. After many farewells, we boarded the KLM plane and jetted into the night bound for Europe.

As we zoomed into space, we discovered ourselves in "the best seats in the house." We crossed the Canadian border while enjoying a delicious supper with cocktails. We chatted with a few fellow passengers including

---

[8] The following pages were edited and transcribed by the author from a portion of her mother's diary written in 1966.

a lady and her daughter who were seasoned travelers. They had just flown from Columbia to America and were bound for Israel. Soon, we dozed off.

When I awoke, I saw an orange streak across the horizon. I knew then we were rushing toward the dawn of a new day. With the dawn, it was easy to see we were far above the clouds. The pilot informed us we were over six miles high and cruising at 585 miles an hour. Every now and then we would come to a break in the clouds where another layer of clouds floated about a mile lower.

Amsterdam

We sighted the lush green land of Ireland, then Scotland. After a delightful breakfast, it was time to fasten our seat belts and prepare to land at Amsterdam airport. After a smooth crossing, we touched down so gently we hardly realized we had landed. Clearing customs took only a few moments. The porter loaded our baggage, and we were off to the city.

Upon arriving at our hotel, we were shown to our spacious, cool and comfortable room. We joined our first excursion into Europe, a sightseeing tour aboard a motorboat on the many canals of Amsterdam. We now understood the term "Flying Dutchmen." Thousands of young, old and entire families ride bikes. We saw sweethearts on two separate bikes with their arms around each other. What impressed us most were ladies riding amidst thousands of cyclists, dressed in the height of fashion, high heels and stylish dresses.

After breakfast we took a plant tour offered by Heineken Brewery. We met a couple there from Whitestone, near our home in Corona, and toured the plant together.

We later visited a dairy farm where they manufactured their own Edam cheese. We were surprised that they milked their cows in the open field from May until October. During the cold months, the cows and other animals lived together in the same spotless brick building. In the barns, the stanchions had been painted snow white and the gutters filled in with hardwood flooring. We could hardly believe we were in a barn.

We left the town of Marken and visited Volendam, where people still dressed in native Dutch costumes and wooden shoes. We encountered an impressive number of people of color and enjoyed greeting them with a nod or quick handshake between the men. Many East Indians, Chinese and others wore their native costumes.

After a leisurely breakfast on Sunday, we visited the Tropical Museum which houses exhibitions displaying various cultures and products of the Dutch Colonies in Asia and Africa, South America, West Indies and the Pacific. It was one of the most interesting museums we visited in Amsterdam. We attended an interpretive dance describing Balinese religious rituals. The dancers were dressed in exquisite exotic costumes. I finally learned how to correctly put on a sarong.

Germany

After gathering our belongings and bidding farewell, we boarded the International Express train, the Lorelie, to Frankfurt. As the train left Holland and entered Germany, we were checked by border guards. Our train proceeded down the picturesque Rhine Valley beside the River Rhine.

In the bustling city of Frankfurt, we went directly to the Auto Europe Agency to settle the details of our purchased car. I spotted a black salesman and believing there would be no language problems, rushed over to him. He was warm and friendly but spoke not a word of English!

We piled our luggage into our Volkswagon and headed for the fabulous, brand-new Autobahn and drove to Austria. After we left the new Autobahn road the town of Strasswalchen at night became quite an adventure due to our lack of proficiency with the German language. We arrived at our hotel after midnight, happy to find the staff not only waited up for us, but also provided us with coffee and rolls. We spent a restful night on lovely soft down quilts.

All along our trip we met fascinating people. One Austrian, a former US WWII prisoner of war, who spoke excellent English, had learned the language during his imprisonment.

By the end of our first week in Europe, we fully realized our good fortune. The bridges our friends built for us to meet their relatives living in Europe provided us with a cadre of acquaintances throughout Europe. We made a quick visit to the home of one such friend and shared a beer.

Beer is the universal beverage in Austria, and an individual bottle of beer is the same size as a family-size bottle in the United States.

At the summer festival in Strasswalchen, we watched the younger crowd dance current American dances until 10 PM when the police escorted those under 16 years of age out the door.

In a German bar one evening, Connie watched her reserved father stand on a table and lock arms with patrons who were singing and cheering. She was shocked! I said to her, "Connie, you really do not know your father."

Summer Memories in Altea: 1973[9]

Once in Spain, Donald and I continued our routine. Afternoons, we drove to the beach and sometimes to a fiesta nearby or in Altea, a small village at the bottom of the mountains. There, a variety of small shops cater to residents and to the many northern tourists that flood Spain each summer. For fun away from the wintry weather in Norway and Sweden, people visit the larger "honky-tonk" town of Benidorm and its family bars.

One day, Rosemarie, our housekeeper, informed us of an upcoming fiesta in Altea near her home. Fiestas were common in Spain, each small village enjoyed community events. Altea's fiesta included a boat race after which observers threw live ducks into the water as swimmers eagerly caught them. Cheers rang out from the fun-loving crowd of spectators.

On Sunday, we left home for Madrid and stopped for lunch at a parador.[10] We drove to the airport early Monday morning. We were so excited to see Connie and the girls, but unfortunately, the New York City Teachers Association's chartered round-trip flight arrived three hours late. The bedraggled family greeted us with smiles and laughter.

Each summer, teachers left New York at the end of June for Madrid or Paris and returned to New York City on the first of September. The teachers' families arrived with tom-toms, guitars, various horns, string instruments and a large group of active children. The plane crew was

---

[9] The following pages were edited and transcribed by the author from a portion of her mother's diary written in 1965. They describe the special and unusual events in my parents' daily lives during their ten year stay in Spain.

[10] Former castles the government has fashioned into hotels. Lovely paradors exist all over Spain, popular with tourists because the rooms are spacious and inexpensive.

irritated by the children playing games, and both children and adults running up and down the aisles.

While waiting to board in New York, Connie chatted with an agitated elderly gentleman in the group who had not wanted to go to Spain. His son explained that his father had not been back to his homeland in 50 years. The son argued that he *should* visit his large family.

The father had left Spain as a young man because of The Spanish Civil War,[11] and desired never to return. He wanted to remain in New York and go fishing on his son's boat. However, when Connie and the girls arrived back in New York in September, the father was elated that he had gone to see his sisters, brothers and the new generation. His family had greeted him at the airport crying with joy.

In Altea, we introduced our family to Ancha, our next-door neighbor from Indonesia. She was charming, welcoming and full of noteworthy social and historical events to share with guests. A remarkable storyteller and great cook, Ancha enjoyed company. She had met her Dutch husband, Karl, once a captive of the Japanese invaders of Indonesia. She risked her life to help him survive the terrible Bataan Death March he and other captive Dutch endured during the conflict. The children listened, enthralled by her stories.

We drove to Alicante, a major city one hour from Altea, to visit the St. Barbara castle. The children decided they would *not* want to live in such a place. The rooms were damp and uninviting.

Spain had recently instituted the unpopular mandatory use of seat bells, but the Spanish police were eager, firm and ubiquitous. Auto drivers invented all sorts of ways to circumvent the law. Ribbons laid across shoulders were hard to distinguish from seat belts. Approaching police officers might have found a fake mannequin doubled up in make-believe pain. This ruse sometimes worked, and the officer waved the vehicle along.

Donald and the grands dropped by our neighbor's house to visit the family's teenaged grandchildren who spoke only French. But no problem, my grands knew enough French to communicate with them. The children

---

[11] The Spanish Civil War widely known in Spain as The Civil War took place from 1936 to 1939. The war is often portrayed as a struggle between democracy and fascism.

spent the afternoon swimming in their pool; and our eldest, Judith, later went horseback riding.

Our young people, along with their new French friends, enjoyed lunch with us in Guardelest. Connie refused to go because the town was at the end of a curving, narrow, uphill mountain road.

Lee Walker, my sister-in-law, and her friend soon arrived from New York City. We drove them to the beach, followed by a barbeque at a friend's house. Judith and I proceeded to a disco that evening. Such a place is truly for young people. Loud! Loud! Judith and I didn't get home until 3:30 AM. Judith claimed I slept at the disco.

During that week we attended a bullfight. If one comes to Spain, one must experience a bullfight. The matadors look dramatic in their attire and swinging red capes, though scientists report that bulls are colorblind. I expected my younger grand, Alicia, to be dismayed by the treatment of the bulls, but she was not.

My grands enjoyed their new friends and kept busy. Lee and Judith visited the flea market. The merchants appreciated my family because they made many purchases of clothing and Spanish souvenirs. An American invited the adults to a party where we danced the night away. What fun!

Telephones were non-existent on the mountain. All who wished to make calls drove to the telephone bank, a series of pay phones in Altea which meant a long wait for an available phone. The frequent promises by the company to install new ones never materialized. Consequently, impromptu visits were constant but welcome.

One morning, we took a wild boat ride in Alicante. The water was rough that day and the boat rocked and rolled all the way to a small island, generally uninhabited. Almost everyone on the boat got

Figure 22 Irma and Alicia at Rastro Don Quijote, Alfaz del Pi, Spain, 1973

seasick. They tried swallowing ineffective seasick pills to no avail. It was quite a sight – a boatload of people vomiting overboard.

Friends and Neighbors

Several of our frequent visitors lived unusual lives.

Mousey, a lady allegedly connected to royalty, had an unhappy role in her native land. She had hidden in Spain. She recounted her exciting experiences to my transfixed grandchildren.

Two lovers enjoyed clandestine visits to Spain while their respective mates remained in England. They did their best to avoid any other English visitors.

Retired Dutchmen related sad stories of being taken captive when the Japanese overran the Dutch Shell Oil community in Indonesia.

Other retirees identified former Nazis they remembered from Germany. "I remember him!" they would say, pointing a finger. Although Spain welcomed Nazis during and after the war, these suspected Nazis were ostracized.

An American named Don Jackson was an important character within our circle of friends. Don was a party man; he entertained, provided dancing music and beverages. When he announced a social event, friends far and wide attended. The party would last into the wee hours of the morning.

Our immediate neighbors purchased a small lap puppy when they left Holland. The dog, Binky, surprised us all because he grew and grew into a large dog that did not realize he was no longer a lap dog. Binky became bigger than his small owner, which provided an on-going comedy for all the neighbors. My grandchildren played with the dog; he visited our house regularly. If his owners were joining us for cocktails, Binky would come along uninvited but accepted.

Spain and France: 1974

The Grands Go to Camp

We planned our trip to France in July to coincide with taking Judith and Alicia, to camp. Both girls were scheduled to spend a few weeks at the Luethi-Peterson Camps organized to foster multiethnic understanding in young people from various parts of the world. The children had an opportunity to fraternize with children they would ordinarily never meet.

When we arrived in Amsterdam rather early the next day, we drove around in a hopeless attempt to find Alicia's camp. We finally gave up and went to a hotel. Connie called around and finally found the locations of the camps. We were looking in the wrong town!

The camp was a well-equipped house on a lake. Alicia happily settled in and gave the administrator her return home plane tickets. Judith's camp for teens in Switzerland expected her in a few days, so all of us planned a short trip to Luzerne. We made sure we knew EXACTLY where Judith's camp was!

We took a boat ride up Lake Luzerne during which I sang a song in Spanish and danced as the orchestra played. Judith and I joined a conga line, and we all had a good laugh. Afterwards at the hotel, we went up to the roof and continued dancing until two in the morning.

Sightseeing

We visited our Spanish neighbor, Ancha's elderly mother, in a comfortable nursing home in Amsterdam. The Dutch government maintained lovely accommodations for senior citizens. She was pleasantly surprised to see us, an American couple who went out of their way to spend time with her.

Our family and New York guests all arrived safely in Altea. Beauford and Connie flew to Madrid to meet Alicia at her flight from camp. The airline ensured her safe pick up. First, they took her to a small room where they asked her if she knew the woman who arrived to pick her up. Alicia explained the woman was her mother. I was pleased to learn the airline took such care of a child flying alone. Fred, the dog, and Alicia were especially happy to see each other.

On Connie and Beauford's last day in Spain, we spent the entire day on the beach with our New York friends. The delightful summer had ended and what a summer it had been! In July, we had traveled throughout northern Europe and in August, we had traveled throughout the south of Spain. We had stayed in top hotels and eaten in the best restaurants. Each day, my Spanish had improved until I was able to converse quite well.

Life could not have been better!

A Surprise Visit: 1975

Daddy, Connie, Judith and Alicia sat on the patio relaxing on a delightful summer day when the bell rang. A surprise visit from a Spanish family.

That evening, we gathered at a finca (a country home) for a paella party to celebrate the traditional Spanish rice dish, and the variations popular in each town or city, including singing and dancing. Afterwards we drove to Alicante to participate in Las Fallas, a fiesta dedicated to St. Joseph. During the festivities "fallas" are burned. These are firecracker-filled, paper-mâché monuments made by the artists, sculptors, painters and other craftsmen of the town. We arrived home early the next morning – what a day.

Connie and the girls arrived near noon from where they had spent the night while the Spanish family was visiting and our guest, Isabel, brought a large live rabbit in a big bag for lunch. I nearly fainted, I begged Isabel to kill it outdoors. Isabel cooked the rabbit and vegetables and made gazpacho, a delicious meal. The whole gang drove to Benidorm where we enjoyed a good flamenco show. We danced in an English-type club and again got home in the wee hours of the morning.

How we met the Spanish family is an interesting aside. Donald, Judith, Connie, Connie's friend Jill and I were driving through mountains when we came upon a sign informing visitors about ancient Roman caves in Carmona. We decided to stop. Unfortunately, the caves were closed for the daily afternoon siesta.

A gentleman appeared and asked us to wait while he obtained the keys. He insisted and told us that black soldiers saved him in some war, and he wanted to reciprocate the kindness, please. I wondered to which war he referred. He returned with the keys and gave us a complete tour of the caves.

Donald offered to tip him or to donate money. "No dinero!" he exclaimed. He invited us to his house. We did not wish to insult him, we followed him to his charming home.

His wife opened the door, "Qué esta pasa?" (What's happening?). Her husband explained who we were. She invited us to stay for a meal. She brought out her daughters' fiesta dresses. Judith and Connie's friend, Jill, had fun trying them on. We took pictures.

A Trip to New York: November 1975

Donald and I were excited about our upcoming visit with the family in New York. Beauford and Connie recently moved into a large house in Upper Brookville, Oyster Bay. In some respects, it was our third home. Their house was large enough to safely accommodate their family of four, Donald and me, and an occasional relative for a short stay.

First, we faced a major problem that needed to be solved immediately. We had to locate someone to keep Freddie, our dog. Many of our neighbors were leaving Spain for the upcoming holidays and did not want the responsibility of a dog. We finished packing, got our flight tickets and boarded Freddy in a suitable facility. The next day, a friend of a neighbor came to our rescue and took Freddie.

I called Connie from the airport. She was shocked to hear we were on our way. We hired a limousine to Connie's house. Connie, Judith and Alicia met us in the driveway. It had been several months since we had seen each other. When Beauford arrived home, he, too, was surprised, but happy, to see us.

I woke early the next morning to fix Alicia a big breakfast and to drive Connie to her college. Donald and I would have use of a car for the day. Later, I dropped Alicia at her skating lessons and picked Judith up from the train station. She would live at home for her first college semester at New York University. We then took Judith to her dental appointment and picked up Alicia from the skating rink. We failed to complete the extensive list of tasks we had composed while sitting on the patio in Spain.

The entire family attended an excellent movie and a great show with the famous kicking and dancing Rockettes at Radio City Music Hall. Beauford and Connie supported a fundraising fraternity dinner dance that night while Donald and I were happy to stay home.

On Monday we drove up to Roxbury – a three-hour drive – and met with our current tenant, a writer. We are contemplating his offer to purchase our house but only a small part of the land. He refurbished the barn as a solitary place to write. While living in the house, he authored a book that became a movie, *The Longest Yard*. The story revolves around prison and the lives of the inmates.

More driving! Donald and I took Connie to the University of Massachusetts, Amherst where she is completing doctoral requirements. We waited for her in the warm cafeteria and read. Connie received a teaching fellowship that covered all fees and required her to teach an undergraduate course in linguistics and reading methods. We are enormously proud of her. Usually, Connie drives the three-hour trek to and from Amherst. Sometimes, she brings third-grader Alicia with her, and they stay overnight at the home of one of the professors.

We saw several Broadway shows including Alvin Ailey Dance Troupe, a famous black classical ballet dance troupe acclaimed throughout the world. What a marvelous show!

Living in Spain, it is easy to forget about rain and how cold New York can be. One night as we stood in line in a parking garage waiting for our car to be brought to us, I heard Donald whisper to Connie, "Don't get any more tickets because I can't stand in this freezing weather and wait for the car one more time." Donald thought I did not hear him, and Connie had a blank look on her face, but we did not go to the theater in Manhattan again.

Thanksgiving

Thanksgiving is here. Donald and I purchased a huge turkey and so did Beauford. Fortunately, the Battys have a spare freezer in the basement.

Beauford's relatives began arriving from Buffalo. They drove seven hours in the rain. Donald and a few of the male relatives took a carload of people to see the Macy's Parade. The rest of us watched it on television.

Figure 23 Holidays in New York
(Donald, Irma, Beauford, Connie)

I always took Connie to see the parade when she was a child, and she continued the tradition with her own children. However, we gave up the hustle and bustle of the mob, the freezing weather and the crowded public transportation to and from the parade. The soft chairs and big television in our den were inviting.

Beauford prepared turkey, stuffing, moussaka, soup, appetizer, tossed salad, spinach, and sweet potato pie. He enjoyed cooking and always prepared a delicious menu for our meals. He joked, "Food does not talk back; if it does not turn out well, it is easy to toss."

That evening we attended the annual fundraising dance sponsored by The One Hundred Black Women, Long Island Chapter. The membership, composed of professional women, raised money to support non-profit organizations addressing the needs of women and families.

We drove Connie to Massachusetts several times. On one trip, Connie discovered she had left her pocketbook somewhere. We phoned everywhere she had been. Much to our surprise and pleasure we discovered that her pocketbook was in a restaurant in New Haven. One of the workers in the restaurant found it. She knew someone would come for it. Donald and I drove the two hours to New Haven in the rain to retrieve the pocketbook. The waitress refused any money. We sent her flowers.

We had not seen Donald's brother, Ralph Wheat, in many years. He had been in the hospital. Donald was pleased to visit him during this trip.

Today it is 15 degrees above zero, but we are surviving. Keeping up with the children is quite taxing. We saw a Christmas program at Alicia's school in which she appeared. Next, we drove to hear Judith's New York University Choir at a concert hall in Manhattan. The concert was delightful. Eighteen-year-old Judith looked lovely in the new dress she had told Connie she did not like when she tried it on in the store.

Connie and Beauford said it was a good thing that we liked the concert because they purchased an expensive dress Judith did not like. Purchased expensive tickets to see the concert, paid a fortune to park near the concert hall and for a congratulatory note to be placed in the concert program, not to mention the expensive family dinner afterward!

Donald's sister came for Christmas. Beauford cooked that big turkey he purchased for Thanksgiving. Judith prepared banana bread and baked macaroni. Donald gave a few words of prayer, stressing how fortunate we are for good health and opportunities to live a rather luxurious lifestyle. The phone rang all day long for Connie, Judith, Alicia and Beauford. It was a busy and happy household.

Connie and Alicia Go Missing: 1977

Alicia and Connie landed in Madrid. Because the next plane to Alicante was hours away, they decided to take the train. On the board listing the trains, they found "The Rapido," scheduled to leave shortly. From the name, they were certain it was an express.

They booked tickets and boarded the train. To their dismay, the stifling train stopped at every station and even places without one. They were waiting in "no place" when another train with closed windows whizzed by. That meant air conditioning. When Connie asked a woman in the compartment about that train, she explained it was for snooty rich people. Alicia and Connie looked at each other and decided that they were snooty and would take that train back to Madrid.

Meanwhile, Donald and I drove to the Madrid airport to pick up Connie and Alicia but could not find them. Worried, we called Connie's friend Peggy in Madrid who told us they took the train from Madrid to Alicante. We returned home and drove to Alicante later in the afternoon. We watched the luggage as it came off and saw the handles of the suitcases where Donald tied red ribbons. We were so happy to see them.

An Extraordinary Year of Traveling: 1978

The Orient

We cruised down the river in Bangkok on the luxury liner Oriental Queen and docked at the gorgeous Oriental Hotel. That night we prepared to travel to Singapore.

Dramamine helped the bumpy plane ride to Singapore. The tour guide met us at the airport and drove us to the Marco Polo, a grand hotel in the city. The next day we boarded a junk (boat) and sailed down the China Sea. Singapore is the fourth largest port in the world, and we saw boats and ships from all parts of the world.

After dinner, a bus took us into Chinatown where a rickshaw carried us into the infamous and notorious Bugis Street, renowned for its parade of hundreds of transvestites who strolled about after midnight. The men, dressed as women, looked like pretty, young prostitutes made up to perfection. People paid double for drinks, but still came out in droves to see the transvestites.

The hotel air conditioning went out in the sweltering heat. Thankfully, we were flying first thing in the morning to Malaysia. I was quite interested in the rubber plantations where they tapped rubber trees for the raw rubber to send to plantation factories. There they made crepe soles for shoes. Several villages nearby supplied housing solely for the plantation workers.

Rarely have we seen black Americans, yet everywhere we go people are friendly. Most of them speak English, so there has been no problem communicating.

Jamaica

In October, Donald and I flew to New York to visit family and prepare for a trip to Jamaica, West Indies. Connie and Alicia would be there for several months. I planned to fly ahead while Donald readied the Roxbury home for sale.

Figure 24 Mother riding a bike on Bugis street

Many passengers brought at least 350 pounds of luggage on the half-empty plane to Jamaica. They brought supplies because of Jamaica's financial problems. Jamaican stores were empty, and the country was in turmoil.

Connie and Alicia met me at the airport. Connie's house could be nice and airy, but because news of robbers frightened her, she wanted the house completely closed for security.

Donald arrived on Tuesday with car parts for Connie's Jamaican friend, Fay. He paid a $40.00 duty fee. He also brought us presents – it was like Christmas!

We dropped Alicia at school the next morning. A wild car ride ensued. We were looking for a podiatrist. Connie would not stop anywhere. I tried to read the map, but no street signs.

Our next adventure to find a bank with safe deposit boxes to rent involved several tries. We found the National Bank of Nova Scotia and put money in the safe deposit box and opened a checking account for Connie and for us to pay our income tax.

During a tour around Kingston, we saw ancient, elegant buildings destroyed in the earthquake of 1692. A humbling experience to see how circumstances beyond one's control can impact lives.

Figure 25 Donald and Irma in Jamaica, September 1978

We rented a house at Ochoa Rios, a port town on the north coast of Jamaica. The rain poured, soon flooding the streets. Connie was afraid to cross the Flat Bridge spanning the Rio Cobre River, a narrow bridge with no guard rails, accommodating a single lane of traffic. That night a heavy rain covered the entire island. We were glad we had turned around.

Instead, we saw a play called *The Jokers*, a satire on Jamaicans. Some of the humor escaped me, but the Jamaicans roared with laughter. We met Connie's friends at a night club and danced and drank.

On Monday, I visited Connie's class of Jamaican teachers. I am happy to see my daughter having such a positive influence on the talented and educated Jamaicans.

Our farewell to Jamaica finally arrived. Friends held a party yesterday for all the teachers enrolled in Connie's class. The spicy Jamaican beef patties and lively calypso music were a splendid send off.

I am so glad we moved around this year, but I am delighted to be at Connie's home spending Christmas with Donald, Connie and our granddaughters in New York.

Chapter Six

Constance J. Wheat Batty: My Life and Times

Early Life: 1947-1960

I attended Flushing High School on Long Island, politically a part of New York City, and operated by the New York City Board of Education. The students who attended lived in Flushing and Corona, New York, and were ethnically and religiously diverse.

During my years at Flushing High School, the teachers of New York City protested the Board of Education. The teachers restricted their activities to teaching classes. Because of the strike, no student papers, sports teams or student clubs continued. The school moved to a split session with morning and afternoon classes. I attended the morning session and rode public buses back and forth to school.

My parents always supported me. When a senior in high school, I mentioned my difficulty in securing an appointment with the busy guidance counselor. My parents made no comments. The next day at school, I was surprised to be summoned to the guidance counselor's office. Upon leaving her office, I was emphatically instructed to inform my father of our meeting.

Figure 26 Constance J. Wheat, age five, 1938

My teen friends and I took a bus to the movie show. Upon exiting the theater, we

47

discovered to our dismay that it was pouring rain. I spotted my father sitting in his car in front of the theater, he had come to our rescue.

As an adult, I developed a greater appreciation of my mother. As a child, I took for granted a clean house, clean clothing every day, weekday and Sunday meals, family celebrations, fun together outdoors, even jumping rope.

In every sense, Mother was my contemporary. In her late teens when I was born, she played outdoors with me. She rode a bike and skated. We liked the same music.

She enjoyed ballroom dancing at parties. She danced with me and made me fancy outfits when I was small. When my Girl Scout troop presented a play I sang, "My Little Blue Gown." Mother designed and sewed a blue gown for me. I believed I was brilliant.

One evening while attending a recital at church, all us children sat in the front row. One of the soloists struck us as hilarious. Every time she hit a high note she stood on her toes. I tried to hide my laughter, I kept looking back at Mother who sat with the other mothers. I tried to hide my snickers and I knew I was in for trouble.

As we walked home, I attempted to explain my uncontrolled laughter to my mother. "How do you think *I* felt sitting with all of those stuffy women trying not to laugh at that ridiculous singer?" She giggled; I was relieved. We hooted all the way home.

Mother always turned the ropes for Double Dutch. Double Dutch requires one person to turn two ropes sequentially and simultaneously. We also played marbles, jacks and hopscotch. Mother was marvelous at jacks. My friends and I always lost when we played against her.

She did the washing in the kitchen on a washboard in a deep tub next to the sink. Big items such as sheets and tablecloths went to a laundry. Outdoor lines extended across the backyard of each house on my block. Mothers evaluated the quantity, neatness and order of items on the line. The frequency of how and when full lines appeared became another topic of conversation. I cannot imagine my mother even caring anything about clotheslines.

Mother learned to sew. She made drapes, dresser scarves and bedspreads. I was proud of my house and invited my Girl Scout troop to hold meetings in our living room.

When my parents purchased their first washing machine, I spent time evaluating this machine, happy to see a button labeled "dishwashing." Since I generally was the dish washer, I greatly appreciated this new piece of equipment. My appreciation diminished, however, when told our family already had a dishwasher – ME!

Mother used a mangle to iron clothing such as the collars and cuffs of my father's shirts and linens. The electric contraption consisted of a large, heated, rotating cylinder. Successful insert of the items required skill, as did retrieving the article before it got tangled in the mangle. Mother became an expert. Ladies would come by to see how a mangle worked. I do not remember seeing such a contraption in the homes of any of my friends.

Although my mother managed the household, she was not interested in being a homemaker. She took a civil service exam because she wanted to get out of the house.

She passed the written office clerk exam and was pleased. Her hours were nine to five which meant she was home by 5:30. It also meant I did not have to come directly home from school each day. This arrangement worked fine for me and for my mother until one afternoon. My father decided to pop home to see how his daughter was getting along. Of course, I was not at home and did not know my father dropped by the house.

Neither of my parents said anything to me at the time, but my mother quit a position she loved. The job became better and better in her mind. She blamed me.

Eventually Mother went back to work, but this time, my parents hired a live-in housekeeper who monitored me. Anna, a Southern black woman, liked my family and I liked her. That program was short lived. My parents and Anna took a civil exam for New York City Courts. I asked my parents why they took the exam because I knew they had no interest in court jobs. My father explained, "Well, your mother sat on one side of Anna, and I sat on the other side. As a result, Anna did well."

Many mothers in our block stayed home. We lived in two-story family houses with small front yards and a larger backyard. A coal burning furnace in the basement heated our house with a fire that needed to often be banked or increased. My mother would suddenly yell, "FIRE!" and race downstairs. Even though my grandmother visited us most days, hearing my mother yell would always frighten her. I would settle my grandmother while Mother tended the furnace in the basement.

We enjoyed the vegetables Mother planted until the day I cut into a tomato containing a great big worm. Afterward, I became suspicious of everything grown in her garden. It was years before I ate another tomato.

As children we played on the porch and weekends, we gathered in one house to listen to *The Shadow Knows*, a spooky (to us) radio program. Most of the children who grew up with me subsequently enjoyed successful professional careers as college administrators, accountants, school principals and teachers. One neighbor became the executive director of a state mental institution.

My paternal grandmother, Leila Davis Wheat, lived across the street and spent time with my mother every day. Mother loved Nonnie. Each day they listened to soaps on the radio, *Stella Dallas*, their favorite. They liked the newscaster Gabriel Heater who began his program with, "There's good news tonight or there's bad news tonight." Nonnie would send me to the store each day to buy one quart of vanilla ice cream (packed by the clerk in the store) and a bottle of cream soda. We each had some, but Nonnie devoured most of it.

In my early teens, Mother's life changed dramatically and forever. My father purchased a luncheonette and stationery store in Corona. Our entire family of four helped to operate the store. During the next two decades, my parents developed and managed an egg and butter distribution business, a small farm with milk cows, became actively involved in politics, real estate repair and sales, hosted entertainment for communities, and not-for-profit community organizations.

Mother, the former housewife, became messenger, secretary, manager, recordkeeper, account manager, companion, co-worker and a constant hostess. She eventually bowed out of housework and hired people to assist her.

As the perfect contributing partner for my father, she was his organized recordkeeper. She ordered supplies for the store, she collected rent, provided lunch for the workmen, and entertained all who came to the door. These skills came naturally to her.

College Experiences: 1950

I do not remember any discussion of finances in my presence, but two new cars for my parents, a new family house and a car for me upon my high school graduation were visible signs that our circumstances had improved. My mother gave me a checkbook as I entered college. She told me to sign her name to the check whenever I wanted money. By my fourth year in college, I knew no one else with that financial arrangement.

In 1950, I enrolled in State University of New York at Fredonia, a small upstate village about 60 miles from Buffalo. I chose Fredonia because of the ski lodge attached to the campus. I envisioned myself gliding down the slopes with vigor and satisfaction as shown in the movies. I had never seen a ski and did not know anyone who skied.

I was disappointed after my first anxious trial practice and ski trip at the lodge. I showed up without ski boots or appropriate equipment and attire. I wondered why the other skiers failed to inform me of the need for these items.

At Fredonia, I met my husband, Beauford Batty, and formed several lifelong friendships. One of those friends, Jeanne, moved to Alaska. While strolling around Anchorage with Jeanne, I noticed people belonging to unfamiliar ethnic groups. Some Jeanne could identify, but some she could not. People dressed for the frigid weather, not for fashion magazines, even at the opera.

Figure 27 Donald, Irma, Connie, Beauford, Batty wedding 1957

Beauford and I married in 1957 and I moved from New York City to Buffalo, where Beauford was born into a large family. We celebrated holidays with siblings, nieces, nephews, aunts, cousins and church members at Beauford's parents' home. At Sunday dinners, enough food on the table provided for anyone who walked in the door.

He taught in the Niagara Falls school system, a 45-minute drive from Buffalo, and I secured a position in the Buffalo School System. Our children were both born in Buffalo.

With the birth of our first child, Judith, my parents came to visit. They walked right past me to see the baby. I burst into tears! I had lost my status as number one, at least in my imagination!

After moving to Buffalo, I overheard Beauford and his friends discussing events shared in high school. Their educational experience was vastly superior to mine. For example, they discussed history and literature about which I knew nothing. My high school left me ill-prepared for this type of conversation.

Figure 28 Connie, Alicia and Judith Batty, c. 1965

When Beauford enrolled at the University of Buffalo, he discovered fellow classmates from private high schools had acquired academic skills unknown to him. As a result of our experiences, we enrolled both our daughters in private schools and their academic development closely monitored by us. Judith was enrolled in first grade at the Park School in Buffalo; and later, both she and Alicia attended the Friends Academy School in Locust Valley near our house.

We lived in Buffalo, New York for the first six years of our marriage. When Beauford accepted a new education position, we moved to Long Island. Our children were educated in expensive private schools, we owned a large house on a five-acre lot on Long Island. Along with my parents, we traveled to many parts of the world. We enjoyed the theater, concerts and dining out. Parties, various lessons – horseback riding, owning horses, skating lessons, and private academic tutors when necessary – were part of our lives. In short, we lived a lavish lifestyle.

Beau spent most of his time working. We had ongoing arguments. Beau had too many jobs: the church organist and choir director, he played at various parties and events on Long Island. In addition, he taught at the NYU Reading Institute, taught methodology to Jewish schoolteachers, and was an adjunct professor at SUNY, City College and Adelphi University. If that was not enough, he catered elaborate parties for friends.

"When you stop spending money, I will stop working so much," he retorted. I finally accepted the fact that he genuinely liked all his jobs.

Beauford and I acquired six college degrees between us. Our lovely daughters, Judith and Alicia (now Alicia Batts) are successful lawyers who contribute to their communities and serve mankind. Both obtained degrees from Harvard, Columbia and two degrees from New York University (NYU). My two grandchildren are enrolled at Harvard and NYU. Wow!

I am proud to see our names listed on the wall in the Smithsonian Institute Museum of African American History: Batty and Batts donors of $100,000. We are blessed to share our gifts with others.

Jamaica: 1978

During January 1978, The Jamaican Ministry of Education invited several American college presidents to a conference in Kingston to plan beneficial international education programs between Jamaica and the United States. Because of this meeting, I was fortunate to accompany the first group of nine Old Westbury students from The State University of New York and to direct the first semester of this program in Kingston, Jamaica. For me, the Jamaican experience began with both the expected, and unexpected.

Beauford and I landed at the Kingston Airport with our daughter, Alicia, during a day of record tropical heat. The airport air conditioner was inoperative that day and by the time we retrieved our luggage and cleared customs, thoughts of aborting the whole venture began to surface! How would I survive in what seemed to be an inferno?

Furthermore, we discovered the word "Batty" was a negative term in Jamaica. Upon looking at our passports, the officials at the gate burst out laughing. I asked them if our pictures were that funny, but no one answered.

The principal at Alicia's school suggested she go by her middle name, Joyce, instead of using Batty. She adamantly refused. She stated, "The others will just have get used to my name. I am not changing it." We later learned that Batty meant "buttocks" in Jamaican.

Beauford confidently drove the small rental car on the left-hand side of the road. What a challenge! At one point he attempted to turn as we do in the States. A group of laughing teenagers on the corner, yelled, "New York driver!"

We drove along the scenic shore road into the heart of Kingston's business district. Goats, cows and donkeys strolling along with Jamaicans. Eventually we located our prearranged living quarters in what turned out to be a seedy motel. The room was hot, small and filthy. A cat had left smelly deposits. I wondered why anyone thought this accommodation would work for a distinguished professor such as myself!

Beauford and I were exhausted but drove to The Pegasus Hotel in downtown Kingston with its pool, dining room, phones, and doormen. We were welcomed as Americans (which there translates as money). The three of us fell fast asleep in the air-conditioned room. The next day we rented a furnished house, accepted a dinner invitation, and the high points of our experience began.

During the first few weeks, after Beauford had departed for New York, I enrolled Alicia in school and made final arrangements for the Old Westbury students' housing, practice teaching sites and orientation. The students lived in a modern hotel/apartment complex on the edge of town. Colorful open food markets and public transportation were within the immediate vicinity of the complex.

The students were involved in a six-day orientation program in which representatives of the Tourist Board, the Teachers Association, the Ministry of Education, and Jamaican Excelsior Education Centre (EXED) participated. The orientation both broadened and enriched the students, especially since many of them possessed little prior experience outside of their monoethnic enclaves on Long Island.

The final plans were completed for the six-credit in-service course I was engaged to teach. One principal and 11 experienced teachers enrolled. The course challenged the participants and me. The Jamaican teachers were not accustomed to attending class at the end of a hot, tiring school day, nor to an informal relationship with a professor. I had never taught in such constant heat, without a textbook (those ordered never arrived) and the unfamiliar deference given to me by the teachers was somewhat uncomfortable. The occasional peddler who wandered into our classroom selling wares created unwelcomed diversions.

The leaders of this newly independent nation recognized the population's desperate needs to raise the literacy level and improve the standard of living. Unfortunately, civil unrest accompanied progress toward this national goal, escalating crime rates, and food and commodity shortages. As the winds of change blew across this island nation, the lifestyles of many Jamaicans were profoundly affected, as well as my own.

Some Jamaicans felt a loss of personal freedom. Social gatherings and evening activities were curtailed. Many were fearful. I had safety concerns, particularly for my daughter, the Old Westbury students and even for myself. The behavior of our adventuresome students, however, indicated they did not share my worries.

Our family's social calendars filled as did my professional calendar. Many Jamaicans opened their homes to my parents, the students, Alicia and me. We drank rum on a veranda high in the Blue Mountains, danced to steel bands along the Caribbean under the Ocho Rio stars, and conversed with fascinating people. Thirteen-year-old Alicia, acquired many friends at school and in the neighborhood, learned some Third World history, and maintained a full calendar of her own.

Picking Alicia up after school was an interesting, multicultural experience. When I needed to locate Alicia at school in Long Island, I would automatically look for one of the few children with my daughter's physical attributes. That technique did not work for us in Jamaica! We found ourselves looking at a large crowd of girls with brown skin, blue uniforms and black briefcases. We chuckled about our new realization and ended up asking Alicia to look for us in a specific part of the parking lot.

Being a faculty member accompanying nine young adult students to a foreign country presented a challenge. In short, I became a surrogate parent! Not only did I resolve the usual mundane problems in student teaching, lesson planning and classroom discipline, but they called upon me to settle financial problems, cooking problems, interpersonal problems, transportation problems and even romantic problems.

I fulfilled speaking engagements at several schools, offered a study skills course to nursing students at EXED and delivered a keynote address at the annual meeting of the Jamaican Reading Association. In each of these instances, I tailored my remarks to meet the unique needs of Jamaicans who functioned in an education system quite different from those systems in the US.

During visits to Jamaican schools and classrooms, I found the educational milieu to be structured, formal and minimally conducive to creative changes by the individual teacher. Jamaican teachers supported my findings by enrolling in my reading methods course. At times, I found myself in a pedagogical quandary. Though anxious to acquaint teachers with well-proven classroom techniques, I felt it a greater value to help them refine skills they could use in their classrooms. Recognizing the impact of an educator such as myself cannot be precisely quantified or measured, I remain confident that the teachers found the course both informative and useful.

The semester went by quickly. The Old Westbury students acquired a sound academic experience and fell in love with Jamaica. The Jamaican teachers expressed positive statements regarding the course, and each earned six SUNY College at Old Westbury credits. Our visiting students were loved both by children and teachers. The teachers who supervised our student teachers regretted our departure. They showed appreciation with farewell parties and small remembrances.

Donald and Irma Wheat were an integral part of this experience. Due to the nationwide unrest, and impatience with the slow progress of needed and promised improvement, some citizens assisted in the redistribution of wealth by robbing stores, banks, houses, buses and other places.

These burglaries necessitated keeping our house completely closed, including the steel door and bars on the closed windows. I rarely let our daughter out of my sight. My parents were in Europe when they learned of my concerns. They left their home and joined me in Kingston. I was greatly relieved. Years later, I learned that my parents were unwilling to spend the hot nights in a closed-up house. After I went to sleep, my father (a large, strong man) opened windows and slept with a baseball bat under his pillow!

The week before our departure from Jamaica, we hosted a pool party for 30 of Alicia's new friends at a major hotel in Kingston. These girls, children of professional parents, had been exposed to many comforts; however, swimming in a hotel pool was a new experience for all of them.

My father transported some of the youngsters, and all planned water games and snacks. The affair was a success!

Alicia met a young man during her stay, and we invited him to join us for dinner at a local restaurant. The meal was served family style with large bowls placed on the table. One bowl contained a quantity of plain white rice. My parents, Alicia and I watched as the young man served himself with three quarters of the rice. We discovered that rice was a major part of his meal, whereas we considered it a side dish.

My family and I left with warm feelings for the people and the land of Jamaica. We, a black American family, were truly pleased to spend time in a country where ethnic differences were not an issue and all the nation's amenities were available to us. In visiting a lovely home in the hills of Jamaica overlooking a posh country club, we noted the number of affluent black Jamaicans riding in golf carts. I compared this Jamaican scene to the one I observed daily at home. I passed private country clubs on Long Island and saw only white people playing golf, occasionally accompanied by a black caddy. I understand the heavy hearts of those financially able Jamaicans who, due to the civil and political unrest, emigrate to other lands.

Oyster Bay, New York: 1975-1992

Each year, my parents flew in from Spain to visit us in Upper Brookville, Oyster Bay. They often stayed through Thanksgiving, Christmas to New Year's Day.

When they left Spain permanently, they moved to St. Petersburg, Florida. Before the family convinced them to give up the long drive from St. Petersburg to Oak Bluffs, Massachusetts, they would stop in Oyster Bay on the way.

Oyster Bay is populated with wealthy people whose homes are situated on five or more acres. My family enjoyed living there, though we were not among the wealthy. We enjoyed the amenities of the Village such as the private police that served the area, the quiet atmosphere and the remote location of our house.

Our first Halloween in the house, we prepared for the treat or tricksters, purchasing bags of candy and cookies. Not one child came to our door.

Our long winding driveway proved spooky to youngsters. One Halloween, I drove Judith to nearby houses, and met other mothers driving crowds of youngsters for trick or treating.

Our wonderful neighbors contributed to our joy. Alicia, my younger daughter, was hired to feed a neighbor's dog when she came home from school. I called the police and informed them my black child would be at the neighbor's house. If the house alarm rang, she accidently set it off. I asked them to note this on their

Figure 29 Beauford Batty at work, 1984

bulletin board. When my parents were visiting, my father always walked with Alicia and remained with her until she came home.

Whenever we entertained, I advised the police that a diverse group of people would be driving around Upper Brookville and may be lost. Several guests told me the police were pleasant and accommodating. Not being there in the summer, we had not installed a swimming pool, but many

Figure 30 Beauford and Connie's
30th wedding anniversary, 1987

neighbors had them. My children and I were free to drop in. In addition, our house was a short walk from the Oyster Bay beach.

During the summers, we rented our house and provided beach permits to the United Nations ambassador from Outer Mongolia. Outer Mongolia is in Asia adjacent to China. We learned about the culture and lifestyles of Mongolians, many of whom were nomads who lived in tents, constantly moving with their crops and livestock.

We notified the police that the ambassador would be staying in our house. One year, an officer from the Brookville Police came to introduce himself and meet the Mongolians. Beaufort opened the door and shook hands with this pleasant officer. The officer assumed my tall, slim, black husband was from the Mongolian Embassy. After the officer left, Beauford and I chuckled. We realized the officer had never seen a Mongolian. When we sold the house, the ambassador expressed his disappointment.

Beauford loved his daughters and me and was always supportive of us. I enjoyed socializing and participated in many organizations. I "dragged" him to events in which he had little interest.

In May 1992, a few months before the gorgeous wedding celebration he and I planned for Alicia, Beau died of multiple melanomas. We had enjoyed almost 40 years of marriage.

That sad event was soon followed by the happy occasion of Alicia's marriage. The day before the wedding, our yard was bustling with people installing the tent, last minute gardening, constructing a platform for band, setting up tables and organizing the catering. We hired a valet parking company since no parking was allowed on Upper Brookville roads.

I walked around to neighbors to alert them to the possibility of some noise in the evening. My immediate neighbors were away for the summer and had rented their house to a recognized politician, a well-known American politician. I had an interesting chat with his then wife, who was, herself, a celebrated news commentator. Their son was three or four years old. Later his mother told me that during the wedding, her child was fascinated by all the drama in our yard.

Figure 31 Judith Batty

Beautiful chandeliers hung in our tented yard. Alicia, in her elegant white Vera Wang gown, walked down the aisle with my beaming father, resplendent in his black tuxedo. We were delighted. Judith, her maid of honor, stood next to her sister at the altar in a beautiful green gown.

The band dedicated *I Did it My Way* in honor of Beauford. He was with us in spirit. Her wedding was the last celebration in that house. I was a widow and now alone. Both my children moved to another state. Noises that were part of the house, now frightened me. This isolated house in which I peacefully lived for decades, now made me anxious.

It was time to leave.

Our Family Grows: 1996

In 1996, my parents and I drove to Virginia to await the birth of my first grandchild and my parents' first great grandchild a robust baby boy arrived as planned. Alicia was thrilled. We took many pictures of each of us proudly holding the new baby. His sister, Emily Batts, arrived three years later in a major

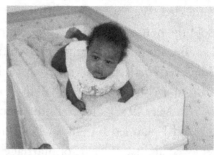

Figure 32 A smiling baby

snowstorm. Although Alicia lived at the top of a steep hill, I was not keen to slide up and down in the snow and ice. We elected to stay in a hotel next to the hospital. It was important that Alicia walk during her delivery, so Daddy walked her up and down the hospital hallway while they chatted. We were teary to think of how fortunate Emily was to have her great grandparents.

Chapter Seven

Donald and Irma Wheat's
Sunset Years: 1980-2010

Winters in St. Petersburg: 1979

For Donald and Irma, who were both reaching their 90th years of life, love, warmth, involvement and activity permeated the 20 years between 1990-2010. Much of each year was spent in St. Petersburg, Florida, and included bridge games, impromptu luncheons, parties, casual gatherings, formal dances, church activities, and fraternal memberships.

Figure 33 Cruising!

Travel played an important part in their lives, with annual Thanksgiving weekend trips to the elegant Greenbriar Resort in West Virginia, occasional cruises, and back and forth trips between Martha's Vineyard, Massachusetts, Washington D.C. and Florida.

Art classes and workshops for Irma, and fishing for Donald were built into their schedules. The family summer house and our Florida houses were adorned with many of my mother's paintings, while our father supplied all of us with fish in every season. Included in their busy schedules were season tickets to attend concerts; plays at various auditoriums; and tailgating parties with friends before major athletic games played by historical black colleges. In addition,

Mother frequently swam laps at the gym and maintained a specific daily goal that she enthusiastically reported to the family.

Irma enjoyed her art activities. She successfully completed a course to become a volunteer docent for the world-famous Dali Museum in St. Petersburg. She enjoyed leading groups of high school students through the museum. Given the erotic nature of Dali's art, the youngsters would ask my mother questions, they believed would be problematic for her. Her responses evoked surprised and embarrassed looks. Mother was in demand to lead these groups as the other docents were reluctant to handle their questions. She was attractive, glamourous, charming and outgoing. She remained that way her entire life.

My mother shared in all Daddy's business plans. She participated in running the store, in real estate management, doing all the paperwork involved with the egg business and the farm, in civic and social organizations, and in raising their children. When my father enrolled in Eckerd College in St. Petersburg, to complete a degree he had started years ago, Mother enrolled in a typing class and typed all his school papers. Truly a dynamic duo!

Increased visits to medical doctors, specialists, dentists, ophthalmologists, water aerobics, golf, computer workshops/practice, and family members' races early each morning to complete the daily newspaper crossword puzzles FIRST – lots of fun – all played major roles in their lives. Naps and rest days gradually became more prominent daily activities. Early in 2002, both parents had cataracts removed. A whole new world opened for Mother as she no longer needed eyeglasses.

Shortly after I moved to Florida, I required a hip replacement. The parents I relocated to Florida to assist were instead taking care of me. We all counted our blessings.

The game of bridge, as well as the social and political aspects involved with the bi-weekly games were organized by 25-30 ladies many years ago when persons

Figure 34 Irma in front of their St. Petersburg home.

of color were not served in Florida restaurants. Thus, the meetings were rotated among members homes. Each hostess arranged an elegant table, prepared delicious meals, appropriate music and service. Members wore chic attire to the bridge games which sometimes included hats and gloves.

When discriminatory practices by restaurants were forced to change, the bridge hostesses arranged lunches and rooms a wide range of restaurant types and various menu prices. For some, the practice of wearing elegant attire to bridge continued.

Irma belonged to a Bonanza game club that met monthly where the hostess served refreshments. Mother's crowd often hosted elaborate meals, including afternoon and evening parties, attended by out-of-town visitors and friends.

My father was an energetic member of the St. Petersburg Alpha Phi Alpha chapter of a national fraternal group. Thousands of black men had become proud Alpha members while in college and remained so during most of their lives. To this day, Alpha men contribute to various local and national charities and participate in a variety of programs assisting young black men. In addition, the Alpha Phi Alpha sponsors an annual well-attended formal dance. Tickets for the dance and the Alpha golf tournaments are frequently sold out.

As an Alpha man, my father encouraged and assisted minority boys to become successful, responsible men. He suggested ways for young black men to safely interact with police and other public authorities. In addition, he served as mentor for a young adult confined to the Boley Center for Behavioral Health in St. Petersburg.

The St. Petersburg mayor selected Daddy to serve on the citizens review board for the police department. As a result, he became well known in the wider community.

Both my parents were active members of the Lake View Presbyterian Church in St. Petersburg. My father was on the church outreach committee which distributed clothing to community families. During this period, he served on the time-consuming nominating committee to select a new minister.

As members of The Northerners Club, a small group of retirees originating from the northern parts of the United States organized fun activities for the members.

Few of their contemporaries owned or mastered the computer, and their friends expressed amazement at the Wheats' proficiency with new technology. Donald recorded information about his stocks using a wireless mouse. Irma played bridge and other games by the hour on their computer and learned how to send pictures.

Their residence was a popular drop-in place. Oranges, grapefruits and lemons were gathered by friends from the trees in the backyard and we held juicing sessions using the elaborate juicing equipment owned by family members. We mailed fruit to appreciative northern friends and family.

Following such a social gathering at their house on 16th Street and 62nd Avenue, my visiting daughter, Judith, after washing the dishes, insisted they buy a dishwasher. The next day her grandparents purchased a dishwasher and marveled they had not thought of that sooner.

One trip during May, the family traveled to Nemacolin Woodlands Resort in the Pennsylvania mountains – it was complete luxury! As I drove through the majestic mountains, my parents enjoyed the sights. However, I was quite nervous due to the height of the mountains and the narrow, curvy roads. When we arrived at the resort, I inquired whether there was alternate route to take home. The pleasant receptionist smiled. All the guests asked her that same question, but she was sorry to say there was no other way. That was our last trip to that resort. Instead, we patronized the upscale Greenbrier Resort in West Virginia for Thanksgiving weekends.

While at Nemacolin, my father took Ian, my eight-year-old grandson, to a fishing contest on a small lake. At the end of the day, a prize was awarded

to whomever caught the largest fish. Shortly after dinner, the manager, a photographer, and a local newspaper reporter arrived at Ian's room with a certificate and a savings bond. He was a happy young man!

From time to time during the winters, traveling Martha's Vineyard friends visited Florida.

Figure 35 Great grandfather reading to great grandchild.

Each year on Valentine's Day, a Vineyard resident would host a large party at her leased home in Sarasota and we all wore red. The men wore big red ties and socks. Most of the 100 guests were Vineyard people. There were lots of hugs and greetings at this joyous, sometime boisterous, gathering.

The Kentucky Derby

Friends invited my parents several times to Louisville, Kentucky, to visit Churchill Downs, spend a day enjoying a Link Party, and watching the Kentucky Derby. The Links are a national social group of professional women of color. The Louisville chapter reserved one floor of the building for their guests to watch the race and enjoy a special dinner with Kentucky mint juleps. Mother prepared special attire for those occasions and was pleased with the many compliments bestowed upon her. All the ladies wore large elaborate hats for the Derby, as is the custom. Watching the race was not the primary attraction.

Graduations

It was customary for the Wheats and Battys to celebrate graduations with joyous family gatherings. Several of the graduations involved unusual occurrences.

The Author's Graduations: 1971-1980

I received a master's degree from Hofstra University in Hampstead on Long Island in 1971, but none of the family attended the services. They were not willing to sit in hot bleachers.

A few years later, in 1980, I received a doctoral degree from the University of Massachusetts. The family arose early for the three-hour drive. The ceremony was lovely, and all watched with pride as I received my Ed.D. My parents treated my family and my dissertation committee to an elegant dinner.

It was the ride home and the choice of radio music that evoked a big argument between my children and my husband. Beauford was a trained classical musician. We had listened to his classical music on the way to the graduation and my daughters wanted something more modern for the ride home. The argument was on!

My father exclaimed, "Stop, you are ruining your mother's graduation." Eventually, all was quiet as Beauford, who was driving, turned the radio OFF.

Daddy Graduates: 1985

Anyone growing up in Donald Wheat's house knew he hoped to finish college. He discussed his wish frequently. During one of my visits to St. Petersburg, a nearby college advertised a new program designed for seniors with college credits and acquired life skills. I mentioned the Eckerd College program to my father. He and I visited the college, a short distance from my parents' house. The staff was accommodating and provided us with a wealth of information and entrance forms which my father gathered up as he prepared to leave.

"Oh, no," I said emphatically. "Pay for it now and enroll in classes!"

He did. It was a significant moment for both of us, his lifelong dream was at his fingertips. Two years and many papers later, he graduated.

May 26, 1985, the entire family was in attendance. It was exceptionally hot that day. I made a quiet personal decision that I would never again be in Florida at the end of May.

Following the ceremony, my mother held a yard party for family and friends. Neighbors, Alpha Phi Alpha men, church people, bridge folks and politicians joined our family to celebrate my father's brilliant success. The weather cooperated by cooling down as people lingered, enjoying the delicious catered food, music and chitchat. My father complained, tongue in cheek, that no one offered him a job now that he completed his degree.

Years later in Florida, my neighbors and I were discussing the Florida weather. I mentioned the heat at my father's outdoor graduation from Eckerd College. One of the ladies, a former employee of the college, said that my father's graduation was the last one held outdoors. The college officers and faculty, equally hot in their academic attire, banned the custom.

Our Daughters' Graduations: 1982-1990

At Judith's New York University Law School graduation in 1982, a gentleman approached my mother, Irma, with "How nice to see you Irma Walker."

Mother regarded him, mystified, "You are mistaken." She had been married so long that she had forgotten Walker was her maiden name. He reminded her that he had been her neighbor when she was a child. They shared many memories.

At Alicia's 1987 Harvard graduation, my mother left the hotel early and rushed to the stadium to reserve seats for the rest of the family. Latecomers, irritated when they could not find available seats, complained. When we arrived, we furtively claimed our precious spots.

At Alicia's Columbia Law School graduation in 1990, we could not win. This time, we huddled together under dripping umbrellas in the pouring rain.

Figure 36 Judith's graduation: Beauford, Judith, Irma Wheat, Connie and Alicia Batty

Thomas Brokaw, the famous news commentator, was keynote speaker. During his address, earlier this year Mandela had been imprisoned in South Africa for leading those fighting apartheid and segregation, had been released. The audience cheered.

Years later when Alicia heard me describing the thrill of Mandela's release at her graduation, she exclaimed, "Gee, Mother, I thought my graduation was the highlight of the event!"

Judith and Alicia traveled extensively for their jobs and for relaxation. Judith was assigned to London, England. She served as General Counsel for ExxonMobil in Tokyo for three years. Alicia, her children and I also traveled to Europe, South America, Asia, the Caribbean and Africa.

Judith and Alicia frequently phoned my parents to keep them abreast of their lives and travels which brought my parents' boundless joy. On December 8, 2006, Mother wrote in her diary, "... I received a call from my Judith visiting the Taj Mahal in India. I was truly thrilled to hear from her. Perhaps I will look for my pictures of India one day... I am so happy to know that my granddaughter is having an exciting life."

Irma enjoyed chatting on the phone. By the time my father picked up the receiver, he did not want the children to run up their phone bills. One day, Judith mentioned Granddaddy was frequently in a hurry and did not want to speak with her. When I mentioned this to my father, he was surprised. Judith and Alicia, unconcerned about money, just wanted to chat. After this exchange, chatting at length became quite common.

My Grandchildren Graduate: 2012-2018

My granddaughter, my granddaughter, celebrated her graduation from eighth grade. The headmistress congratulated the class and reminded the youngsters they were expected to acknowledge their achievements and to sit quietly as young men and ladies with hands resting in their laps and legs together.

Her comments fell on deaf ears. Most of the young ladies in their graduation dresses sat whichever way they were comfortable. Emily was one of the few girls who followed the head mistress's suggestion. She rose and walked gracefully across the stage in her new high heels to receive her diploma.

Figure 37 Irma enjoying a cruise

A few years later, an elegant Emily, who spent her senior year of high school in Italy, walked across another stage and joyously joined her United States classmates to receive her diploma.

My grandson, Harvard class of 2018, was the second great-grandchild to celebrate a graduation without Donald and Irma present, though we all felt they were there in spirit.

It was a three-day ceremony. I immediately noticed that the crowd appeared to be comprised of parents my daughters' ages. Was I to be one of the few grandparents? The next day as I sat in the lobby, I saw a large truck stop in front of the hotel. The door of the truck opened. When the many wheelchairs rolled out one by one, I knew grandparents were on the scene.

What a marvelous childhood my grandchildren, continue to experience. Emily attended her senior high school year in Italy. Ian spent several months in Indonesia in a precollege program.

Chapter Eight

A Year of Unusual Events: 1996

The Delegates Elected

Irma Wheat's diary entries document this remarkable year. She begins with a description of St. Petersburg's evolving political scene at a rowdy delegate voting meeting in March.

Out of the many candidates, Donald and I were elected delegates to the 1996 Democratic National Convention in Chicago. Our friends, politicians, neighbors and church members rallied their support.

Lakeview Presbyterian Church was filled with more than the usual members this June. Photographers and newsmen from the *St. Petersburg Times* wrote about the few racially mixed congregations in the Deep South, especially in Florida.

The newsmen and photographers showed particular interest in Donald and me as delegates to the Florida Delegation of the Democratic National Convention (DNC) of 1996 in Chicago. Writeups and pictures of us appeared in Florida and Chicago newspapers. We proudly sent copies to family and friends around the country.

William Clinton and Al Gore wished to meet the needs of the country's population, both black and white. This stance appealed to Democratic delegates. Several state delegations declined to participate in the convention because blacks were involved as delegates, and instead organized their own groups outside the DNC.

Mississippi carried out systematic methods of prohibiting black voters. The state had denied voting rights for generations with poll taxes, literacy and comprehension tests administered by white agents. Employment threats were common to blacks who served white families. The state's democratic party traditionally limited participation to whites only.

Beginning in 1961, organizations waging campaigns to register blacks encountered violent opposition preventing them from enrolling many black voters. The unusually harsh treatment used by police with dogs and water hoses while gleeful whites and their children looked on provided instant worldwide news reports and photos.

The longstanding political, economic and social events that contributed to the raucous delegate meeting in St. Petersburg were those experienced by individuals and groups in other areas of the South. Descendants of 1000s of black slaves who worked on cotton plantations and in white-run industries continued to demand equal rights. In many areas, these descendants outnumbered the whites. This statistic alarmed many whites who believed blacks were subhuman and not entitled to opportunities as US citizens. Moreover, whites realized their political and economic powers could be threatened. Many local and national papers supported these concerns.

In 1981, the Florida Statewide Democratic Party Convention in Hollywood, Florida, stressed the need to increase the power and influence of black Democrats within the party. History had been made on September 24,1983, when the Florida Democratic Party recognized the Democratic Black Caucus of Florida (DBCF) as an official organization. DBCF chapters were established statewide with the clear mission to sustain, maintain, and gain black power in all aspects of Florida life. However, lack of common goals at the 1995 St. Petersburg Democratic Party created tension which dominated that meeting.

In 2013, Dr Darryl Paulson, a retired professor of history at the University of South Florida, detailed how the state permitted only whites to vote in the primaries and denied access to anyone who could not read. Furthermore, lengthy residency requirements were a condition for voting. The *National Voting Rights Act of 1965* outlawed many discriminatory voting practices, yet contemporary scholars assert the vestiges of denied voting rights remain.

Headlines in Florida complained that legislators were making it harder for black citizens to vote. After Congress passed the 13, 14 and 15 Amendments, many states developed strategies prohibiting poor whites and all blacks from participating in government. Convention delegates needed to be registered voters. Throughout the southern states, real obstacles prevented black registration.

Various strategies were used between 1870 and 2013 to obstruct or prevent poor white and black voters from casting ballots. For example, in 2011, Florida officials reduced the number of hours of early voting, thus giving persons working day jobs little or no time to vote.

The Wheats go to Chicago

In this vibrant setting, we left for the 1996 Chicago Democratic Convention. August 24 was the big day. We boarded a small plane and were met in Boston by a pleasant woman holding a board with WHEAT and YANCEY written on it. Once in Chicago, we took a bus to the lovely Palmer House. Traffic was heavy, a parade objecting to something held us up.

On Saturday evening, a welcoming party for the delegates took place at the Navy Pier. Information regarding Chicago, the convention, and the history of Democratic conventions overwhelmed us. Thirty-five thousand attendees were projected to utilize complimentary shuttle transportation to and from all airports, train stations and hotels.

Thousands of attendees would pack United Center's 18,231 seating capacity. The Chicago '96 Committee was responsible for producing hospitality events, including 56 delegation parties and a welcoming party for 15,000 representatives of the national and international media.

We were up early to obtain our credentials for the day. Officials carefully verified personal identification for admission. Hundreds of people milled about waiting for credentials. We listened to speakers upon speakers, Governor Lawton Chiles and Senator Bob Graham of Florida among them.

In time, we boarded a crowded bus to the convention center. The bus filled with cheering, excited folks wearing unbelievable costumes. Everyone was in party mood. We arrived at the Center and found excellent seats. By evening, cold and tired, I returned to the hotel where I planned to take a brief nap before attending an affair that evening. When I awoke, it was morning. Donald was also asleep. No party that night for us!

The next morning, we received our credentials, and joined a group going to the Chicago Celebration restaurant where an excellent fundraising brunch had been organized by the Beulah A. G. Smith Scholarship Foundation. This organization supports an enriched education for black children. We felt honored and pleased.

During the brunch, a Chicago newspaper called to make an appointment for an interview. Donald and I were among the oldest delegates and one of few delegate couples in one of the earliest racially mixed Florida delegations. The reporter feigned shock when we proudly revealed we were both 82 years old and married 64 years. Clearly, we were newsworthy!

After lunch, we boarded a bus back to the convention hall. The buses were plentiful – we never waited. Many excellent black and white speakers of both genders addressed the crowd. Governor Mario Cuomo delivered a speech; Jesse Jackson, introduced by his son, Jesse Jackson Jr., gave his usual rousing lecture. I was exhausted. We planned to attend an evening affair at the Noor Pier. Donald escorted one of the ladies in our delegation while I rested at the hotel.

We knew the convention center would be packed on the final day. As usual, I ran ahead of Donald to save seats. Gore and Clinton gave stirring acceptance speeches. Thousands of balloons and silver confetti floated down from the ceiling as Jesse Norman, a world-famous black soloist, sang. Thousands of happy people cheered and hugged one another. The excitement was palpable! That night, we attended a party for the Florida delegates and fell into bed late, late, late.

We had a great time in Chicago. So many parties, entertainment, delicious food, friendly people. Clinton and Gore were now successful candidates for President and Vice President of the United States.

After an uneventful plane ride back to Martha's Vineyard, Connie met us at the door to inform us that we were on television. She received calls from friends excited to see us on the news.

We returned to our busy life. I joined the Polar Bears for a cold, early morning swim. Connie came later, and we all felt rejuvenated. I brought newspapers with our pictures at the convention. They were a hit! As we relaxed on the porch, our granddaughter, Alicia, called to tell us our one-year-old great-grandson, Ian, looked at a picture and readily identified us. "G-G and Papa!" We were thrilled.

★ ★ ★ ★ ★ ★ ★ ★ ★ ★ ★ ★ ★

VOTE FOR

DONALD and IRMA WHEAT
As Delegates to the 1996
DEMOCRATIC NATIONAL CONVENTION

VOTE   VOTE

Democrats let Donald and Irma Wheat represent you at the

Democratic National Convention in Chicago to be held August 26 - 29

They are a remarkable team, married for 64 years, who have together served their Community with outstanding distinction.

IF YOU ARE A REGISTERED DEMOCRATIC VOTER IN SOUTHERN PINELLAS COUNTY (CONGRESSIONAL DISTRICT 10) YOU CAN VOTE TO SEND TO CHICAGO TWO PEOPLE WHO WILL REPRESENT YOUR VIEWS AND HELP TO RE-ELECT PRESIDENT CLINTON AND TO ONCE AGAIN ELECT A DEMOCRATIC CONGRESS.

DATE:
SATURDAY
MARCH 30, 1996

TIME:
10:00 A.M. to 2:00 P.M.

PLACE:
PLUMBERS AND
STEAMFITTERS HALL
4020 80TH AVE. NORTH
PINELLAS PARK
1/2 BLOCK WEST OF U.S. 19
1/4 MILE NORTH OF PARK BLVD.

Always working together
Pinellas County Democratic Executive Committee- Affirmative Action Officer
Florida State Democratic Convention - Delegate 3 Times
Inner City Major Political Action Committee (IMPACT) President
Voter Registration Drive- Outstanding Service Award from Democratic Party
Tampa Bay Regional Planning Council Area Agency on Aging - Volunteers
Community Police Council - St. Petersburg, Member 10 years
Campaign Manager for the late Morris Milton for State Legislature District 55
Alpha Phi Alpha Fraternity, St. Petersburg (A service organization) Member - Secretary
United Way Allocations Board, St. Petersburg
Lakeview Presbyterian Church - Elder - Choir Member
PARENTS — GRANDPARENTS — GREAT-GRANDPARENTS

FOR MORE INFORMATION CALL 864-1018

Figure 38 Delegate Voting Flyer, 1996

Chapter Nine

Summers in Martha's Vineyard: 1977

Around 1977, some friends invited our family up to Martha's Vineyard. Beauford dragged his heels. He said, "Oh, that place is full of snooty people, I don't want to go."

We finally visited them over the Labor Day weekend. We met people on the boat to the Vineyard and partied with them all weekend without the kids.

The following summer we rented a house for a month, the year after, for the entire summer. My parents soon followed and bought a place in 1978. Their sojourn in Spain was over.

The home my parents purchased in 1978 is remarkably different today, the house has a wonderful location – one house away from the popular Oak Bluff town beach – close to the post office, grocery stores, restaurants, and fancy clothing and beauty shops. When purchased, this residence had no closets, only one-and-a-half bathrooms, minimal electricity, no washer and no sewers.

When guests came, the several loads of laundry took up three machines at the public laundry. My mother's friends were welcomed, but she insisted they bring their own sheets. One insulted friend told Mother she

Figure 39 The Wheat Home on
Martha's Vineyard, 2019
(Image by Peter Graves)

had never heard of bringing one's own sheets in all her travels. She never came to visit and wasn't missed.

A friend says, "Winter is just something to get through until one can begin life anew on Martha's Vineyard." I agree. I like the sense of community, the ambience, and I love entertaining on the porch.

Journalist Jill Nelson in *Finding Martha's Vineyard* quoted my description of our island days. Beauford established a Sunday tradition; after church, friends would come by for hors d'oeuvres and a Bloody Mary. We always had a full porch. I did not feel covert or subtle racism on the Vineyard, though I was ever on guard. My children were safe here; and as teenagers, they experienced almost unlimited freedom. That was not the case on Long Island. (Nelson, 2005)

Prior to our arrival one spring, and to my father's displeasure, we purchased a stair chair. "Get rid of it," he complained.

I refused to remove it. I never heard another word from him. Now, over 30 years later, I'm the one using it.

My parents always drove from Florida to the Vineyard. They stayed in the Carolinas for one night and at Judith's DC apartment for a week or so. On the way, they saved quarters to do her laundry, much to Judith's pleasure. Now her very modern kitchen has up-to-date appliances including a washing machine, dryer and a built-in coffeemaker. My father was exhausted when they arrived at his granddaughter's house in DC, and more exhausted by the time they reached the home of Long Island friends, Hermine and Robert Lewis.

Various health issues emerged in my parents' lives. They did not share their concerns with family members, but Mother wrote about them in her diary. When driving between Florida and the Vineyard became a challenge, they sent boxes to the Vineyard by UPS and took the sleeper train to DC. The sleeper train proved unsatisfactory; the sleeping quarters were unpleasant and too small. Neither one of them was able to sleep.

Eventually they honored the family's request not to drive the three-day trip, to fly instead. My father complained to everyone who passed by the Vineyard porch. "My children insisted that I leave my car in Florida. Now, I do not have my tools to fix things," he grumbled. He did not get the response he expected. Many friends agreed with his children which was difficult for my father to hear. My father never had anything repaired by others. He fixed everything himself. As a child, I followed him and watched him work.

Oak Bluffs

Oak Bluffs is one of five settlements on Martha's Vineyard. The houses along Narragansett Bay were built in the mid-1800s without indoor heating. Whaling captains built these large summer homes for their families. Many have a widow's walk on the roof. This "walk" is a small addition at the top of the house where wives could look out over Narragansett Bay and watch for their captains to come home.

Today, Oak Bluffs is an ethnically diverse community. Every race, religion, and economic level are well-represented there, and on the entire island. The town is one of the oldest African American vacation destinations in the US. Prominent people of color have purchased homes or regularly vacation on Martha's Vineyard, including performers Paul Robeson, singer Ethel Waters, Oprah Winfrey, Spike Lee, Beyoncé and Jay-Z, composer Harry T. Burleigh, and others. Adam Clayton Powell Jr., one of the first African American congressmen, and Barack Obama and his family are frequent visitors.

Neighbors who summered on the Vineyard for 30 or 40 years, welcomed us into their circle of friends. We enjoyed fun-filled summers with them. These days, my college-aged grandchildren often come with their buddies.

Around 2004, Judith and Alicia refurbished the house and installed a large basement. This construction entailed lifting the house onto stilts to reconstruct the foundation and add cooling and heating. The new recreation area contains audio/visual equipment, tables and sofas, and games. We now have six bedrooms and six bathrooms. An up-to-date kitchen with an attached sitting room adds a modern touch. Despite the air conditioning, on nice days we still relax on the porch.

Figure 40 Summer Party on the Vineyard, September 1987

A decorator helped my daughters purchase furnishings. My father did not live to see the finished house. Mother lived to enjoy the attractive and useful amenities of her new home. The place constantly overflowed with family and friends. Even today, my children and grandchildren fill the house with overnight guests.

My parents, both avid readers, enjoyed engaging in serious discussions with friends. Donald and Irma read the local newspaper as well as St. Petersburg's *The Weekly Challenger*, news and information for the African America communities around Tampa, Florida. They subscribed to *Ebony* magazine, *Readers Digest* and the AARP magazine. Both liked reading James Baldwin's books. Current events conversations for men, were held weekly at the Oak Bluffs Community Center. My father held court with his appreciative contemporaries, sharing his wide and noteworthy life experiences.

The arrival to the Vineyard was filled with expectations. Phone conversations bubbled with excitement: "When is so-and-so arriving?" "How was your winter?" "What are your kids up to?" Topics included new babies, marriages, deaths, graduations and, of course, "When is the next party?"

The Cottagers, Inc.

The Cottagers, Inc. is a summer organization of 100 black women homeowners on Martha's Vineyard. These women, key contributors to the Island's social life, purchased and maintained a building, Cottagers Corner, for their activities and meetings.

During the summer, the organization sponsors a community yard sale, a clam bake, informal dances and parties, a tour of historic houses, and an African American Cultural Festival. The events are open to the public and are well attended by the community.

The Cottagers hold an annual fashion show and luncheon, a major affair of the season. My glamorous mother modeled an assortment of beautiful beach, church and formal attire loaned by nearby owners of retail clothing shops.

The Cottagers offer art classes for children, dances for teenagers, bridge lessons for adults and lectures of interest to the African American community. Notables such as genealogist Dr Henry Louis Gates Jr of *Finding Your Roots*, James Comer from Yale and other black faculty from Harvard and Princeton have been guest speakers and participants.

The organization contributes monetary donations to the Oak Bluffs fire and police departments, the library, the hospital, and to programs serving the needy. The Cottagers also award scholarships for graduating seniors from Martha's Vineyard High School.

My Mother, the Social Butterfly

Mother loved being a part of my group of friends. However, my friends felt inhibited when she joined our gatherings. They respected her as an older woman and felt they had to watch their language and stories. I introduced her to activities where she could participate independently. I wanted her to find her own companions.

In 1979, Mother became a painter while summering on Martha's Vineyard. Delilah Pierce, an art instructor at Howard University, volunteered to teach art at Cottagers Corner. I urged Mother to join her classes. Delilah encouraged her to paint regularly.

Neighbors recognized Mother's talent and bought her paintings. Her artwork adorns my condo walls both in Florida and Washington DC. Her works also decorate her granddaughters' homes.

She soon found other groups to join. Each morning, local ladies walked together. Sometimes, I joined them. Within a short time, my mother would be striding along far ahead. I found it difficult, if not impossible, to keep up, always ending at the back of the group.

Neighbors driving by or riding bikes would wave and make amusing comments. "Your mother is way ahead of you. Go, Connie, go!" My ineptness was displayed for the world to see. I quit!

One fall, Mother required hammertoe surgery. After surgery, she found herself shut-in and off her feet. She received phone calls from family and friends who feigned shock to find her at home.

The senior center quickly scheduled summer lunch dates and card parties planned by the women. The men organized golf parties. Mother and I planned 18th hole parties for my father's golf friends. The gentlemen, unconcerned about the party ending, came, ate and stayed.

Wives called late in the evening asking for their husbands. "Don't tell me he's still there!"

Island Teens

Most people buying second homes on the Vineyard were financially stable. I wanted my children to meet other children of similarly privileged backgrounds. Alicia was in her early teens when we first arrived on the Vineyard. She established friends quickly. Judith, already in college, visited on weekends.

My parents and I were fortunate to witness two sets of teens grow up: my daughters and their friends and, 25 years later, their children.

Figure 41 Irma Wheat and her paintings

Teen parties for my grandchildren, called a "Batt Bash," took place in the furnished basement where partygoers could enter and exit through a private entrance. Word spread around the teen crowd that our house was the place to party. Parents joined the fun from neighboring porches and appreciated the flow of adult drinks. In case a problem arose, they were on hand to provide adult supervision. At one party, we entertained a special guest, the elder daughter of President Barack Obama. The secret service personnel sat discreetly on our porch.

I am in the end of my eighth decade of life. Watching these extraordinary young people grow up was a privilege. Our house was full every day. Now and then a young friend stops by to give me a shout. I am always delighted.

Healing Waters

The well-attended opening of the Oak Bluffs Polar Bears, held each year on the Fourth of July weekend, commences with a blessing. Everyone is happy to see returning friends and is eager to begin the Polar Bear ritual.

The season ends on Labor Day weekend with a prayer for continued good health.

Every Monday, we shared a potluck breakfast on the beach provided by Polar Bear members. When Donald was alive, he would buy a big box of sausages from a wholesale restaurant supplier and cook them all. My mother beamed with pleasure among the joyous crowd.

Hearty laughter rang out after breakfast as we jumped into the frigid water. Shrieks of pleasure broke the early morning silence. "This is delicious!" "I must be crazy to be here this time of the morning!" "This water is freezing!"

Folks formed a circle and joined in a workout led occasionally by my mother. Others swam from jetty to jetty, while the timid sat on a bench to watch. The only qualification for membership was to show up. What a wonderful way to begin the day!

Eager summer swimmers still gather by the water around 7:30 in the morning. Participants come from different directions. Some walk, some ride bikes, and others drive. Swimmers chitchat then eventually head for the healing waters of Narraganset Bay.

A few kibitzers claim they *will* go into the water one day; but for some, that day has not yet arrived. They come for the fellowship and to participate in the ritual by fetching buckets of water for rinsing sand, holding towels and gossiping.

The Polar Bears often attract the interests of passersby. One woman asked my mother in all seriousness, "Do you ever see Jackie Kennedy on the Island?"

Figure 42 Polar Bears Potluck Brunch

My mother promptly responded, "Oh yes, frequently, whenever we hang clothes on the line!"

Enthusiastic Polar Bears sport sweatshirts, T-shirts and towels with "Polar Bears" emblazed in big letters. One morning, while wearing my shirt in a nearby shop, the proprietor inquired, "Are you one of those famous Polar Bears who jump into the freezing water each year on New Year's Day?"

"No way. I'm a member of the Martha's Vineyard Polar Bears. We swim and exercise from June to Labor Day."

"Where do you swim?" he asked.

"We swim right here in the Bay."

He looked at me in surprise. "I pass those people each day on my way to work and I thought you were praying or baptizing people!"

When I told the other Polar Bears, we all had a good laugh.

Why are we Polar Bears drawn to the water year after year? Many swimmers speak of the healing water. Members tell of the aches and pains soothed and the energy restored by the water. The bracing dip jumpstarts their day.

Figure 43 The Polar Bear Club of Oak Bluffs

We validate one another, celebrate the joy of life, and respect each other as individuals. It is our fellowship, love and friendship that carries each of us through the long winters.

The Beach Bench: 1981

In the early 1980s, The Friends of Oak Bluffs organized a fundraising project where engraved benches were sold to the public. That winter, I purchased one to be placed on the main avenue adjacent to the waterfront at the end of the block near our house. I wanted my parents to see the bench while they were alive.

As we arrived on Narragansett Avenue the following summer, I could see the bench. I drove toward it and stopped. I pointed out the new bench and wondered aloud, "Who put that bench there?" I asked my dad to get out and look at the plaque. He looked mystified but consented. A big grin crossed his face when he read the plaque.

My mother jumped out to see why my father looked so happy. There written in elegant lettering was my tribute, "This bench is donated in honor of Donald Wheat and Irma Wheat by their daughter Dr. Constance J. Batty."

They hasten to inform their visitors and guests of my homage. It is clearly visible from our porch, so Mother would joke, "Look at those people sitting on our bench." Today, many dedicated benches line the waterfront.

Fishing

Daddy enjoyed fishing from the beach, the dock and from the commercial fishing boat. He frequently brought his great-grandson with him. My parents packed freezer chests so the entire family could enjoy it most of the year. They would frequently stop to replenish the dry ice as they drove home to St. Petersburg.

Mother and I did not fish, but Mother knew countless ways of preparing seafood. Summer meals, including breakfast, often consisted of some type of seafood.

My father once caught an enormous eel. We knew not how to prepare it. We wondered if we even wanted to prepare it. When we told our neighbor, Mrs. Dowdell, about our huge eel, undaunted, she came over to assist. It is unfortunate no pictures were taken during this operation! An interesting string of events occurred.

Other neighbors dropped by to observe. Mrs. Dowdell, a tiny senior citizen who knew about everything under the sun, and my father, a large man in every way grappled with the slippery, wet creature. My father held the eel with a tight grip while our diminutive neighbor stood at the other end of the eel, gradually slicing and pulling the tough skin from the eel. When the eel was fully skinned, it was sliced as one would slice a banana. The small pieces were fried slowly for a few minutes. The more adventurous neighbors tasted it and were delighted. They said it tasted like chicken.

The Portuguese American Club members, sponsored Friday all you-can-eat fish fries. These Portuguese Americans mostly hail from Cape Verde, a former Portuguese colony located near the western coast of Africa. Many reside on Martha's Vineyard the entire year. This private club contains a bar and they rent their hall for Island social events. Our family often patronized the fish fries and enjoyed the fellowship that came with the meal.

When my children were small, I planned a luncheon for 12 of my friends. Everything was prepared and ready to go when my father arrived unexpectedly with 13 three-pound lobsters and a chef. The planned menu of tuna-salad-stuffed tomato was happily augmented, much to my surprise and joy. On her way to the hospital to give birth, my friend, Loretta, stopped by, saw the lobster, and pleaded with me to save one for her. She gave birth to a healthy baby girl and later claimed her lobster.

Yard Sale-ing

As the balmy weather cooled, the time to depart approached. My parents went "yard sale-ing" every Saturday. Beach chairs, golf clubs, beach umbrellas and floats, children's toys and clothes, porch furniture and other items were sold or given away by people leaving the Island. Mother and Daddy, both artistic and handy, purchased any number of items that needed fixing. Prior to updating, our small cellar became crowded with interesting stuff.

Porch Sitting

Porch sitting and entertaining remain part of the Vineyard lifestyle. Friends express how pleased they are to sit on the porch in "Paradise," the name Vineyarders use to refer to Martha's Vineyard.

If neighbors pass any house where no one is on the porch and the doors are closed, they assume no one is home. After our house was air-conditioned and when it was very hot, our porch-sitting time diminished.

Neighbors and friends would knock on the door to find out if anyone was home. Because of the noise of the air conditioning, the radio, the television set, the stereo,

Figure 44 Don and Irma on the front porch, c. 1988

I could not hear the knocks. I eventually installed a doorbell, the only one on the street.

In 1997, my one-year-old grandson, Ian, visited the family on the Vineyard with Jennifer, his babysitter from Virginia. Ian delighted in his many trips to the parks and to the giant merry-go-round, but best all, he liked the beach, the water and playing in the sand. He enjoyed his pails, shovels, beach balls and his special beach shoes.

My father installed a swing on the porch which became a magnet for small children. He attached a long rope which made the swing easy to swing the children. We love seeing the delight on my grandson's face as

he swung back and forth. What fun that was for everyone, both the swingers and the watchers.

Near the end of the season, the fire department sponsors a major firework show in a park around the corner from our house. People come from all over

Figure 45 Ocean view from the front porch

the Island and Cape Cod to see the fireworks. We do not venture into the crowd; we can watch from our porch.

Because our house is so near the fireworks, not only do friends come to sit on our porch, but also, they call the day before to request use of our driveway.

Before five o'clock in the evening, surrounding streets are crowded. Drivers ferrying impatient visitors search in vain for parking spots. Others push strollers, wheelchairs, and ride skateboards as they look for places to sit.

When the show begins, streets around our house are closed off to all traffic. Friends munch on snacks and sip favorite drinks while watching the display.

The Summer of 1985

During the summer of 1985, my daughter Alicia enrolled as an intern in a Connecticut firm. She invited fellow interns to our Oak Bluffs home for a weekend. They arrived with sleeping bags, party and beach attire.

Judith and Alicia fixed a big breakfast of cheese grits, sausages, fish, pancakes and orange juice for everyone. We were all accustomed to fixing food for a crowd. My father sat on the porch watching and listening to these stimulating young people. The breakfast lasted until early afternoon when the youngsters left for the beach.

When they cleared out, Alicia asked my father about two boys who were not a part of the intern group. He explained that he saw these young men heading for the beach, assumed they were Alicia's guests, and wanted to eliminate any breakfast stragglers. He told the boys in no uncertain terms that breakfast was being served *now*. The young men were surprised but enthusiastically joined everyone at the dining table. This incident demonstrated the community ethos prevailing at Oak Bluffs. Father invited two young men to breakfast who felt comfortable enough to join the crowd and partake of our food and fellowship.

Mother's Cancer: 1996

My parents were at the stage in life where they required frequent medical care and attention. The topics of ailments and medicine dominated many conversations. That summer, mother was diagnosed with breast cancer. I dropped off and picked up my parents at the ferry. American Cancer volunteers met her (sometimes with my father) at the Falmouth dock and drove her to Cape Cod Hospital for her off-island infusion shots and treatments. She continued her active life, as well as following her doctor's orders.

Despite her illness, my mother celebrating her 82nd birthday in Florida on March 15, 1996. The group of ladies in her spa class held a luncheon at a Pinellas Mall restaurant and presented Mother with a scrumptious birthday cake decorated with lovely pink flowers and a picture of a glamorous lady. That evening, my parents attended the annual formal fundraising dance given by the St. Petersburg graduate chapter of Alpha phi Alpha fraternity.

The ladies take pride in wearing outstanding outfits to these affairs and making a grand entrance. My mother wore an orange, silk, flowing gown that conjured up wealth and excellent taste.

Mother was pleased she did not have bad reactions from the treatments other than occasional fatigue. She played bridge several times a week and sometimes walked to the beach where we sat in the same spot year after year and talked with the same acquaintances about ourselves and the world. My mother's behavior was the topic of conversation. She seemed unfazed by the cancer and the treatments. Her friends found this baffling. She would come home from her cancer therapy and go off to a party that evening.

Gracious volunteers drove them back and forth to the hospital. These trips became the highlight of my mother's visits to the hospital. When we returned to Florida in the fall, we mailed each volunteer a large quantity of oranges from our yard.

When Mother learned her younger brother, Leon, lay deathly ill in a Pennsylvania hospital, my parents were able to secure a flight. Leon was thrilled to see them. Mother had cared for Leon during much of their childhood and felt close to him. After a brief visit, she and Daddy returned to the Vineyard and planned the next trip to the Cape Cod hospital for Mother's treatment.

My parents entertained many guests from St. Petersburg and Long Island during August, high season on the Vineyard. The Cottagers, Inc. sponsored a concert at Union Chapel, the local summer church. The singers, Dot Saunders and Barbara Fitz, were my parents' houseguests. In the evening after the crowded concert, The Cottagers held a reception for the singers at the Cottagers Corner. Their visit was a pleasant distraction from Mother's medical routine.

In between the Polar Bears on the beach, bridge lessons at Cottagers Corner, manicures, pedicures, lunch and dinner dates, bridge parties, and chatting on the porch, my mother attempted to relax.

On August 22, I picked them up from the ferry after Mother's morning cancer treatment. By mid-afternoon we were on our way to the sailing camp for the Cottagers' Annual Clam Bake where they served lobsters, clams, potatoes, cold slaw, clam chowder and all the fixings. My mother participated in any activities the Cottagers organized, and this event was no exception. They presented a skit, provided dance music, and distributed the door prizes donated by local businesses and individuals.

This year, when the fire department gave their annual fireworks show, instead of sitting on the porch, my parents watched the show from their bedroom balcony dressed in their night attire.

Chapter Ten

The Death of Donald Wheat: 2004

The death of my father in January 2004, was a trying period for the whole family. My parents and I were traveling to St. Petersburg when we stopped for a few days at my apartment in DC to spend time with our children and grandchildren.

My father decided to take a bath while I was out. He slipped and fell on the bathroom floor. He was a big man, and Mother and I could not pick him up. I called the front desk for help. When the female security guard arrived, we realized additional aid was needed. My father was embarrassed to be seen without any clothing and lying on the floor.

We called for an ambulance which came with a full complement of paramedics and police. They helped Daddy up as Mother supplied a robe. On the advice of the paramedic in charge, he was taken to the hospital.

We visited him each day. He was lucid and able to have an ongoing conversation with us. Ultimately, an ambulance brought him back home to my apartment. The stretcher would not fit into the elevator, so the staff supplied a wheelchair. Quite an ordeal.

At our last Christmas Day family dinner, we arranged an elaborate meal at Judith's apartment. She hired a nurse and an ambulance to transport him to her apartment where we were joined by two of her lifelong friends, both medical doctors. We enjoyed this precious time with him, and Judith's friends appreciated the opportunity to spend time with my father whom they had known since childhood.

Back in my apartment, his condition deteriorated. He was not talking, eating or drinking. The Washington DC Hospice staff provided my father with homecare to make him comfortable. In time, we moved him to the hospice facility. He understood it was appropriate for him and the family. He passed away shortly after being admitted. My daughters, my mother and I were with him. After Daddy's death, Mother and I continued our drive to Florida. There we planned final ceremonies for him and a dinner for guests.

Following his death, friends came to relate stories about my father. Yom Bolling, our young neighbor on Martha's Vineyard told us how Daddy called him over and said, "Thank you for being so nice and helpful to my family. I won't be back next year, and I want you to know how much your assistance is appreciated."

I look like my father. Both at the Vineyard and in St. Petersburg, strangers still stop to convey anecdotes about him. I dined with a family friend who worked with Daddy in a church program organized to collect and distribute clothing to needy people. She shared that Daddy had been the organizer and manager of the effort. I did not know that.

A service was held at the Lakeview Presbyterian Church filled with friends and family members, with standing room only. A sit-down dinner was served in the ballroom at Point Brittany Condominiums. A breakfast for our out-of-town guests followed the next morning at the St. Petersburg Yacht Club.

During the dinner, Judith showed a video featuring my father in various stages of his life. It was clear to us all how much love and respect the community held for him. One elderly guest, unknown to family members, came in a wheelchair with his helper. He explained that as a youngster he lived in the apartment building my grandparents had built in Corona adjacent to their own house. What a pleasure it was for my family that this elderly and elegant man came to pay his respects and to demonstrate his love for the Wheat family. We were happy to see that he possessed the good fortune to retire in Florida. Many aged black Americans must work until their deaths.

Chapter Eleven

Irma Lucille Wheat Relocates: 2008

My father's passing in 2004 resulted in many changes for our family. Mother continued her fun-filled life until 2008, when she became unable to keep up with the house. Her penmanship declined and she no longer could write in her diary. Furthermore, she stated she was *finished* with cooking.

When she decided not to stay in her house, we helped her make new living arrangements. We located College Harbor, an assisted senior citizen facility in St. Petersburg familiar to Mother where several of her friends lived. We encouraged her to stop driving after an incident where she became lost while driving. The College Harbor staff and I were available to take her everywhere. Mother reluctantly agreed.

She played bingo, read the paper, watched television and was with me part of each day. College Harbor operated a bus for residents to enjoy tours of the town or rides to concerts or restaurants. I joined her on many of these excursions.

I relocated and moved into a condominium close to Mother. We were in constant contact. We phoned, visited, dined and took short trips together. She was often at my condo where she enjoyed the pool and my water aerobics class. Unable to follow the routine of exercise, she remained in the pool walking and exercising her arms and legs. My neighbors in the pool enjoyed chatting with her and held her in high regard.

Figure 46 Irma Lucille Wheat, c. 2008

Mother and I attended Lakeview Presbyterian Church where she sang in the choir. She was very devoted to the church and members frequently visited her.

Mother enjoyed her life in Florida and her summer trips with me to the Vineyard, though without my father's supervision moving these days from Massachusetts to Florida presents challenges. The porch needs cleaning, furniture needs to be taken indoors. We now leave one car at the Vineyard covered for the winter.

We used to shut off the telephone, electric and water, and rerouted mail. Now we leave the utilities on and put the television, phone and internet on seasonal rates. It is less trouble to leave everything on low rather than return the following spring to wait days for reinstallation. Utility companies are overwhelmed by the number of "snowbirds" demanding service.

Friends would come by to wish us safe travels to Florida and some goodbye cocktail parties and gatherings occurred as we prepared to leave Martha's Vineyard. Mother preferred driving rather than taking the trains. I would drive to New London, Connecticut, then take the two-hour trip on the cross-island ferry to Long Island as Mother napped and read the paper. We were fortunate to have good friends on Long Island with whom we spent one or two nights.

We typically returned to St. Petersburg in mid-October where friends welcomed us back. Mother rejoined her clubs and the general pace of life at her senior assisted living quarters.

From 2007 until 2010, we spent each summer at the Vineyard. Friends and family came to visit, and though her memory was not always up to par, Mother recognized most of the guests.

Union Chapel is at the end of our street, and in prior summers, Mother walked to church. Now, Mrs. Williams accompanied her to the Chapel on Sundays. Only open during the summer months, visiting ministers provided the services.

The Death of Irma Wheat: 2010

Years before, my mother had become worried about her mind and had written about it in her diary. She indicated her computer was not working properly, that she missed my father's help. We both noticed her penmanship was changing and the quantity of her writing each day was diminishing.

On June 22, 2010, her last entry reads, "We are here in Martha's Vineyard watching television."

In July, I took her to her doctor and was shocked to hear him say, "Irma, you've been here a long time. Don't you think it's time to go?"

My mother replied, "Yes." I was unsure if she heard him correctly.

The doctor recommended home hospice care. It wasn't long before her hospice nurse recommended Mother go into a nursing home in Falmouth, a ferry ride away. The family spent all afternoon with her on her last day. She talked and chuckled with us. She died in her sleep at the Falmouth Care and Rehabilitation Center on August 9, 2010. She was 96.

We held a celebration of her life at Union Chapel; the church was at full capacity. We served a meal at our house attended by my friends, Mother's friends, Judith's and Alicia's friends, family members, Polar Bears and bridge players. Mother enjoyed a long, remarkable life, loved and happy.

Figure 47 Union Chapel, Martha's Vineyard.
(Image by Peter Graves)

Epilogue

Authoring this book has been a most meaningful experience. Reading my mother's diaries, reviewing long letters sent to me during my parents' travels, listening to tapes they recorded about events that impacted their lives, and sharing my life with them, provided me with a deep understanding and knowledge of Donald Louis and Irma Lucille Walker Wheat.

I knew them to be intelligent, determined, loving and inspirational during their lives and mine. They began their extraordinary lives with few assets, in a world where opportunities for black people were limited. They nonetheless successfully met many challenges.

They left footprints as they travelled in many circles of mankind. Their knowledge and understanding improved the lives of people surrounding them. They received numerous awards and much recognition. They were especially pleased to have been personally invited to the Inauguration and Inaugural Ball of William Jefferson Clinton, President of United States.

Devoted to family, they made a positive impact on four generations. They were known as Mother and Daddy, Grandmother and Granddaddy, GG (Great-Grandmother) and Pop Pop (Great-Grandfather). The entire family enjoyed extensive travel to various parts of the world, including Asia, Africa, the Caribbean.

While the Wheats enjoyed successes, many of their plans and decisions were marred by racism and the color of their skin. My father's ability to work had been overshadowed by the difficulty to gain employment as a fireman in New York City. Once hired, he faced hostility and resentment from the other firemen.

When my father retired, the South was hostile to people of color, so moving to Florida was not an option. Black people demanding their civil rights faced massive resistance, abusive treatment and death threats.

Living in Spain provided my parents with a minimum of overt discrimination. Still they faced questions implying, "What are you doing here?" and "How did you get here?" My children were asked, "Is your father in the army?" When Judith was seven years old, a hotel guest asked, "Where is your father stationed?" She did not understand what the lady meant, and replied, "My father is not stationed."

The Presidential Inaugural Committee
requests the honor of your presence
to attend and participate
in the
Inauguration of
William Jefferson Clinton
as
President of the United States of America
and
Albert Gore, Jr.
as
Vice President of the United States of America
on Monday, the twentieth of January
one thousand nine hundred and ninety-seven
in the City of Washington

Figure 48 Invite to Clinton/
Gore Inauguration, 1997

We saw few African American families traveling in Europe and never saw any big families traveling with a baby, or youngsters traveling with parents and grandparents. Our family was the topic of conversation wherever we went.

Together we created memories to sustain us for the rest of our lives. We have role models who continue to form our life decisions. We have a sense of purpose gifted to us by the love this dynamic couple shared with each one of us. We pass down a legacy that can change the world.

Footprints and Legacies

CITY OF NEW YORK
DEPARTMENT OF HEALTH
BUREAU OF RECORDS AND STATISTICS

Borough of **QUEENS**   New York, N. Y.

Below is a photostatic copy of a certificate on file in the Bureau of Records
and Statistics of the Department of Health of the City of New York.

Certificate of Death

Certificate No. ___156-61-412634___

1. NAME OF DECEASED   *CLARENCE*   *WHEAT*
   (Print or Typewrite)   First Name   Middle Name   Last Name

PERSONAL PARTICULARS	MEDICAL CERTIFICATE OF DEATH
(To be filled in by Funeral Director)	(To be filled in by the Physician)
USUAL RESIDENCE (a) State **New York**	16. PLACE OF DEATH:
(b) Co. **Queens** City or Town **Corona**	(a) NEW YORK CITY (b) Borough *QUEENS*
(d) No. **111-24 Northern Blvd.,**	(c) Name of Hospital or Institution *111-24 Northern Blvd*
(e) Length of residence or stay in City of New York immediately prior to death **50 Yrs.**	(If not in hospital or institution, give street and number) (If in hospital, give Ward No.
SINGLE, MARRIED, WIDOWED, OR DIVORCED (write the word) **Widowed**	17. DATE AND HOUR OF DEATH (Month) *Oct.* (Day) *28* (Year) *'61* (Hour) *1030*
DATE OF BIRTH OF DECEDENT (Month) **February 26th,** (Day) (Year) **1888**	18. SEX *MALE* 19. Approximate Age *7C*
AGE **73** Yrs. If under 1 year mos. days If LESS than 1 day hrs. or min.	20. I HEREBY CERTIFY that (I attended the deceased)* (a staff physician of this institution attended the deceased)*
a. Usual Occupation (Kind of work done during most of working life, even if retired) **Retired Pullman Porter**	from *1 30 19 55* to *10 35 19 61*
b. Kind of Business or Industry in which this work was done **New York Central Railroad**	and last saw h *im* alive at *11 30* M on *10 35 19 61*
SOCIAL SECURITY NO.	I further certify that death *was not* caused, directly or indirectly by accident, homicide, suicide, acute or chronic poisoning, or in any suspicious or unusual manner, and that it was due to NATURAL CAUSES.
BIRTHPLACE (State or Foreign Country) **Atlanta, Georgia**	* Cross out words that do not apply.
OF WHAT COUNTRY WAS DECEASED A CITIZEN AT TIME OF DEATH **U. S. A.**	† See first instruction on reverse of certificate.
WAS DECEASED EVER IN UNITED STATES ARMED FORCES? **no** 10b. IF YES, Give war or dates of service	Witness my hand this *3rd* day of *October* 1961
NAME OF FATHER OF DECEDENT **Unknown**	Signature *Hugo Alexander* M.D.
MAIDEN NAME OF MOTHER OF DECEDENT **Unknown**	Name of Physician *HUGO ALEXANDER* M.D. (Print or typewrite)
	Address *25-06 94th*

NAME OF INFORMANT	RELATIONSHIP TO DECEASED	ADDRESS **Hard Scrabble Rd.**
Donald Wheat	**Son**	**Roxbury, Del. Co., New York**
13. Name of Cemetery or Crematory **Flushing Cemetery**	14b. Location (City, Town or County and State) **Flushing, New York**	14c. Date of Burial or Cremation **November 1st., 1961**
5. FUNERAL DIRECTOR **O. P. Armwood**	ADDRESS **101-04 Northern Blvd., Corona 68, N. Y.**	

BUREAU OF RECORDS AND STATISTICS   DEPARTMENT OF HEALTH   THE CITY OF NEW YORK

This is to certify that the foregoing is a true copy of a record in my custody.

CARL L. ERHARDT   BY
Director of Bureau   Borough Registrar

Figure 49 Clarence Wheat Sr. Death Certificate

99

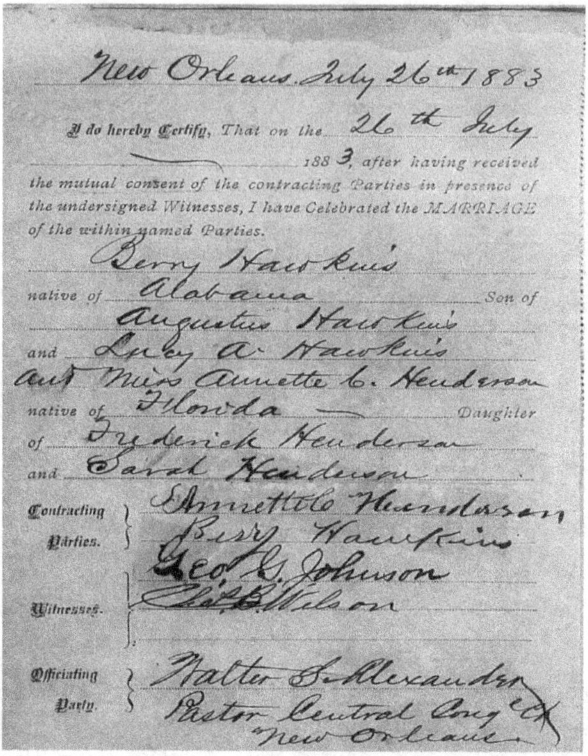

New Orleans July 26th 1883

I do hereby Certify, That on the 26th July
_____ 188 3, after having received
the mutual consent of the contracting Parties in presence of
the undersigned Witnesses, I have Celebrated the MARRIAGE
of the within-named Parties.

Berry Hawkins

native of Alabama   Son of

and Augustus Hawkins
and Lucy A. Hawkins

And Miss Annette C. Henderson
native of Florida   Daughter

of Frederick Henderson
and Sarah Henderson

Contracting } Annette Henderson
Parties.   } Berry Hawkins

Witnesses.   } Geo G. Johnson
             } Wilson

Officiating } Walter S. Alexander
Party.   } Pastor Central Cong. Ch.
                  New Orleans

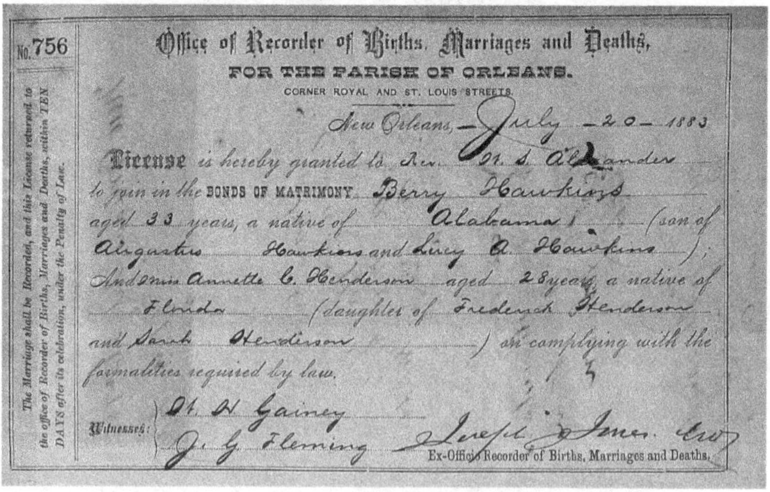

No. 756

Office of Recorder of Births, Marriages and Deaths,

FOR THE PARISH OF ORLEANS.

CORNER ROYAL AND ST. LOUIS STREETS.

The Marriage shall be Recorded, and this License returned to the office of Recorder of Births, Marriages and Deaths, within TEN DAYS after its celebration, under the Penalty of Law.

New Orleans, July 20 1883

License is hereby granted to Rev. W. S. Alexander
to join in the BONDS OF MATRIMONY Berry Hawkins
aged 33 years, a native of Alabama (son of
Augustus Hawkins and Lucy A. Hawkins);
And Miss Annette C. Henderson aged 28 years, a native of
Florida (daughter of Frederick Henderson
and Sarah Henderson) on complying with the
formalities required by law.

Witnesses: W. H. Gainey
            J. G. Fleming   Ex-Officio Recorder of Births, Marriages and Deaths.

Figure 50 Marriage Certificates of Berry Hawkins and
Annette C. Henderson. (New Orleans)

100

Page: 4

S. D.: 1 ; E. D.: 154 ; Minor Civil Division: 2nd Ward.

From Schedule No. 1									
House No.	Family No.	NAMES OF SURVIVING SOLDIERS, SAILORS, AND MARINES, AND WIDOWS.	Rank.	Company.	Name of Regiment or Vessel.	Date of Enlistment.	Date of Discharge.	Length of Service.	
1	2	3	4	5	6	7	8	Yrs. Mos. Days	
41	367 367	Petrium Victor alias Daakus J. Fw.	Private	B.		Aug 22 1867	Aug 22 1870	3	41
42	353 355	Daakus Asa	Private	I.	25 Reg Inf	1863	1866	2 3	42
43	408 408	Hodges Hilbert	Corporal	E.	80 La Inf	1863	1866	3 6	43
44	400 400	Miller Harris				186	186		44
45	343 343	Turner Alfred	Private	E.	96 La Inf	1863	1866	3 6	45
46	414 414	Hawkins Augustus	Private	E.	87 La Inf	1863	1865	2 6	46
47	412 412	Fagan Wiley	Private	I.	7 La Inf	1864	1867	3	47
48	358 358	Johnson Charles	Private	I.	11 La Inf	1863	1866	3 3	48
49	352 302	Alexander Adam	Private		80 La Inf	1864	1867	3	49
50	255 300	Louis Joseph	Private	C.	4 La Cav	1862	1864	2 8	50

POST-OFFICE ADDRESS.	DISABILITY INCURRED.	REMARKS.	
10	11	12	
41 Ashton Plant.			41
42 Ashton Plant			42
43 Hapoza Plant			43
44 Hahnville, La		Could not get my facts as to Length of	44
45 Madisonville			45
46 Taylor Plantation			46
47 Taylor Plan		All of the above Ex Colored	47
48 Ashton Plant		Soldiers	48
49 Ashton Plant			49
50 Ashton Plant			50

NOTE.—The provision of the act of March 1, 1889, under which this special enumeration of survivors of the war of the rebellion is made, reads as follows:

That said Superintendent shall, under the authority of the Secretary of the Interior, cause to be taken on a special schedule of inquiry, according to such form as he may prescribe, the names, organizations, and length of service of those who had served in the Army, Navy, or Marine Corps of the United States in the war of the rebellion, and who are survivors at the time of said inquiry, and the widows of soldiers, sailors, or marines.

The entries concerning each survivor or widow should be carefully and accurately made, so that the printed reports may contain only thoroughly trustworthy information.

Spaces are provided on this special schedule for the entry of fifty names, or, more properly, terms of service. The spaces are numbered consecutively from 1 to 50, and cover the four pages comprised in each schedule. The inquiries made concerning each survivor or widow call for the repetition of the number of the house and family as returned on the general population schedule (No. 1), the name, rank, company, regiment or vessel, date of enlistment, date of discharge, and length of service (in years, months, and days) on the upper half of each page, and the post-office address, disability incurred, and general remarks on the lower half of each page. The column headed "Remarks" is intended to be used to cover any points not included in the foregoing inquiries, and which are necessary to a complete statement of a person's term of service in any one organization.

In the case of persons having served in more than one organization, use as many spaces as may be necessary to cover their various terms of service. In the case of widows of deceased soldiers, sailors, or marines, make the entry of her name on the dotted line, as follows: Mary J., widow of Brown, James H.; filling out the record of his service during the war, and giving under "Post-office address" the present address of his widow.

Figure 51 1889 Special Census, Augustus Hawkins, Taylor Plantation, Louisiana

Figure 52 *Freedman's Bank Records, 1865-1871, 1872*

Figure 53 The Savoy Ballroom 1926-1958
(Image by Emily Batts)

MASSACHUSETTS HISTORICAL COMMISSION
Office of the Secretary, State House, Boston

In Area no.	Form no.
F	10-77

4. Map. Draw sketch of building location
   in relation to nearest cross streets and
   other buildings. Indicate north.

* and unusual balustrade.

1. Town_ Oak Bluffs

   Address 12 Narragansett Avenue

   Name

   Present use Private seasonal dwelling

   Present owner Olivia J. Steele

3. Description:

   Date   1875

      Source Tax records

   Style   Campground

   Architect

   Exterior wall fabric cut and plain
                        wooden shingles
   Outbuildings (describe)

   Other features Two covered balconies
   with pierced board brackets and
   double doors. Pierced board barge
   boards on one of the gable dormer
   Expansive covered post & bracket
   porch with two decorative pedimen
   Altered   Date

   Moved   Date

5. Lot size:

   One acre or less   X   Over one acre

   Approximate frontage   39'

   Approximate distance of building from stree
                   10'

6. Recorded by Jill Bouck

   Organization Oak Bluffs Historical

   Date   Survey   Aug. 11, 1978

(over)

37M-7-77

103

7. Original owner (if known)_____Mrs. K.P. Kingman_____

Original use__Seasonal private dwelling_____

Subsequent uses (if any) and dates_____

8. Themes (check as many as applicable)

Aboriginal		Conservation		Recreation	X
Agricultural		Education		Religion	
Architectural	X	Exploration/		Science/	
The Arts		settlement		invention	
Commerce		Industry		Social/	
Communication		Military		humanitarian	
Community development	X	Political		Transportation	

9. Historical significance (include explanation of themes checked above)

    This house is significant as a part of the original Oak Bluffs
Land & Wharf Co. Development which began soon after the growth and
popularity of the Wesleyan Grove Campground. It became the secular
alternative to the Campground, and flourished as one of the most
popular and well known East Coast summer resorts. The house is of
the expansive Campground architecture.

10. Bibliography and/or references (such as local histories, deeds, assessor's records,
early maps, etc.)

Evalutation Records, Town Hall, Edgartown, Mass.
Oak Bluffs Town Assessor's Maps, 1975.
Henry Beetle Hough, Martha's Vineyard, Summer Resort, 1835-1935.

Figure 54 Massachusetts Historical Commission, Oak Bluffs House

Figure 55 *MV Magazine*: Great-grandson Ian Batts fishes with great-grandfather Donald Wheat. (Vineyard Vacations, Inc., 2004)

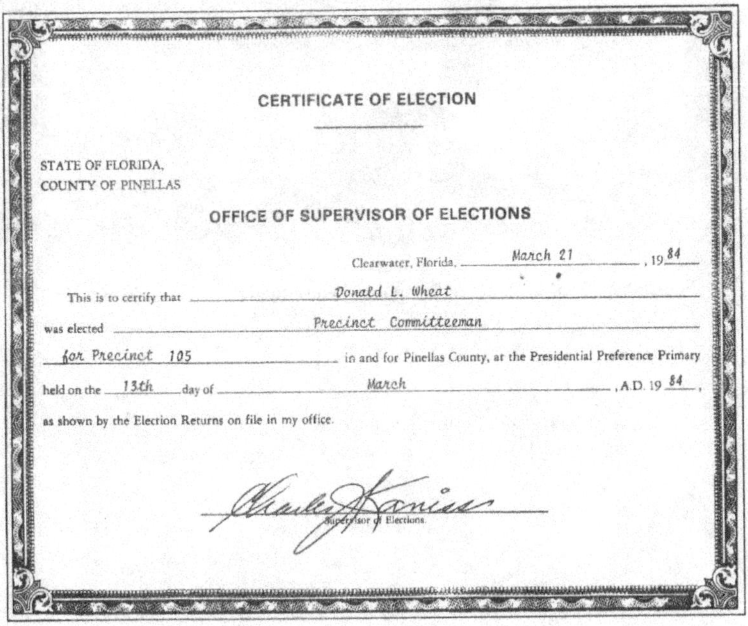

CERTIFICATE OF ELECTION

STATE OF FLORIDA,
COUNTY OF PINELLAS

OFFICE OF SUPERVISOR OF ELECTIONS

Clearwater, Florida, _____March 21_____ , 19 84

This is to certify that _____Donald L. Wheat_____

was elected _____Precinct Committeeman_____

_____for Precinct 105_____ in and for Pinellas County, at the Presidential Preference Primary

held on the __13th__ day of _____March_____ , A.D. 19 84 ,

as shown by the Election Returns on file in my office.

_____Charles Kaniss_____
Supervisor of Elections

Figure 56 Donald Wheat Precinct Committeeman, 1984

CERTIFICATE OF RECOGNITION

presented to

DONALD WHEAT

Whose volunteerism has been instrumental to the
Tampa Bay Regional Council
Area Agency on Aging
in providing essential quality services to elders.

April 11, 1997
Date

Sally D. Gronda, Director

1962

Figure 57 Donald Wheat, Tampa Bay Certificate of Recognition, 1997

Figure 58 Various Paintings by Irma Walker Wheat

Figure 59 Certificates of Appreciation, Irma Walker Wheat, 1997

Donald Wheat, 89, Was Businessman and Mentor

Donald L. Wheat, an active citizen of Oak Bluffs and St. Petersburg, Fla., died peacefully on Jan. 13 at his daughter's home in Washington D.C., seven days before his 90th birthday.

Mr. Wheat, son of the late Clarence and Leila Wheat, spent his early years in Corona, Long Island, New York. He attended the public schools of New York city and was graduated from Stuyvesant High School, the elite, honors high school in Manhattan. Mr. Wheat became one of the earliest African-American firemen for the city of New York and was instrumental in founding the Vulcan Society, which was composed of African-American firemen and was designed to promote equal opportunities for all New York city firemen. In addition, Mr. Wheat was a businessman who, along with his wife, owned and operated a successful luncheonette and stationery store in Corona. Mr. Wheat promoted and sponsored many social events for the community and was instrumental in bringing many well-known entertainers and artists to the Long Island community. As a business owner, he was a mentor to many young men while employing some of them and served as discussion leader for local youths interested in business and politics. Mr. Wheat served as a committee chairman for the Democratic Club and as president of the Corona chapter of the National Association of Colored People.

Mr. Wheat retired from the New York city fire department and he and Mrs. Wheat moved to Roxbury, N.Y. Roxbury at that time was a farming village where Mr. and Mrs. Wheat purchased a 150-acre dairy farm. It was in Roxbury that Mr. Wheat, along with his wife, started and developed a major wholesale butter and egg bonded trucking business. Wheat's Eggs Inc. purchased eggs from chicken farmers throughout the city. During these years (1950s and early 1960s) there were no other African-American egg dealers bonded in the state of New York.

In 1962, the Wheats lost their only son, Donald Jr., seven years of age, in a tragic auto accident. Mr. Wheat took his wife to Europe for a few weeks to gather strength and to regroup. This trip grew into two years of extensive travel around Europe and Africa. When the Wheats returned to the United States, Mr. Wheat accepted a position as supervisor for a fire insurance underwriting agency. In this position, once again, Mr. Wheat mentored many young African-American males who had been recently hired by the company. This supervisor/mentor position became a 24-hour responsibility for Mr. Wheat.

Ultimately, in response to friends from Europe and at the urging of his wife, the Wheats returned to Europe, purchased a villa in Spain and remained there for seven years. Each year the Wheats returned to the United States to celebrate the Christmas and New Year holidays with their family, and their family sojourned each summer to Spain. These were exciting years for the family.

During the last 25 years of his life, Mr. Wheat lived in St. Petersburg, Fla., and Oak Bluffs. In both places, his services as an active and responsible citizen were exemplary. He served several terms on the St. Petersburg police review board and as an elder of the Lakeview Presbyterian Church. Mr. and Mrs. Wheat represented St. Petersburg as delegates to the National Democratic Convention in Chicago when former President Bill Clinton was nominated. Mr. Wheat served as a campaign manager for several candidates seeking political office in Florida. He was an active member of the St. Petersburg chapter of Alpha Phi Alpha Fraternity; in that capacity, he was particularly interested in assisting young men prepare for college. In addition, he was active with the local St. Petersburg Democrat organization and served on various committees. Also while in Florida, Mr. Wheat volunteered as a guardian for several Boley residents and monitored the phones for the council on aging. The Wheats were members of the St. Petersburg Yacht Club. Mr. Wheat also found time to complete his bachelor's degree at Eckerd College.

While in Oak Bluffs, Mr. Wheat was an avid fisherman and bridge player. As a fisherman, he supplied his family with fish for the winter. As a bridge player, he was a charter member of the Martha's Vineyard chapter of the National Bridge Association. He belonged to the "Polar Bears" and participated in many programs sponsored by the Oak Bluffs Council on Aging. He was also a member of the Mink Meadows Golf Club.

Donald Wheat is survived by Irma, his wife of 72 years; his daughter, Dr. Constance J. Batty of St. Petersburg; two grandchildren, Judith Batty Esq. and Alicia Batty Esq. of Washington, D.C.; a sister, Mrs. Ruth W. Miles of New York city, and a host of nieces, nephews and friends. Two children, Judith and Donald, predeceased Mr. Wheat.

The family suggests contributions in memory of Donald L. Wheat may be sent to Pinellas County Urban League Inc., 333 31st street North, St. Petersburg, Fla. 33713, and to Hospice of Washington, D.C., 4200 Wisconsin avenue NW, Washington, D.C. 20016.

Health Plan Meeting

The board of directors of the Island Health Plan will hold its annual meeting and a public reception at 5:30 p.m. on Monday, Jan. 26, at the Mansion House Hotel meeting room in Vineyard Haven. The program will feature a roundtable discussion with guest speaker Jim Hooley, CEO of the Neighborhood Health Plan.

Figure 60 Donald Wheat Obituary (Vineyard Vacations, Inc., 2004)

Alpha Tribute To Donald Wheat
MEMORIAL SERVICE

Does any Human Being realize life while he lives it.....Every, Every minute? Thornton Wilder, in his play, OUR TOWN, examines this question. In the Play, Mr. Wilder takes his audience to the local cemetery where Emily, the Protagonist, now deceased, begs the stage manager for one more chance to experience life. Once her wish is granted, she finds the people she loves most, moving along at a frantic pace, missing out on the nuances of life. It is then that she asks the stage manager this penetrating question: Does any human being realize life while he lives it....every, every minute? After some pondering, the stage manager replies: "Saints and Poets, maybe they do....Some." Don Wheat was a unique blend of both saint and poet, for he knew the essence of life. Though aware of his mortality, he was also aware of his opportunity for Immortality – and he grasped it.

He was a plain soft spoken man who spoke with courage of his convictions, never prone to self indulgent oratory. So mild was his demeanor that few of us were aware of the magnitude of the quiet giant who walked among us. He was meek - but never timid. He was, in the true sense of the word – a gentle man. He was a visionary with a passion for youth. While some saw obstacles and difficulties, Don Wheat saw challenges and opportunities. And so, we need not to idolize or enlarge him in death any more than we did in life. For, in actuality, Don Wheat delivered his own eulogy through his day - to-day interaction with those of us who were fortunate enough to know him.

Individually, we are richer, but in a larger sense, the world is a better place because Don Wheat left his footprints on the sands of time. As an Alpha man, he represented the very best among us. For he was what we wish we could be. Surely, Shakespeare must have had an image of Don Wheat in mind when he penned these immortal lines; "His life was gentle and the elements so mixed in him that nature might stand up to all the world and say: *THIS WAS A MAN*'."

Figure 61 Alpha Tribute to Donald Wheat

Dear Brothers of Alpha Phi Alpha:

YOUR PRESENCE AND PARTICIPATION AT THE MEMORIAL SERVICE FOR MY FATHER, DONALD L. WHEAT , WAS VERY, VERY MUCH APPRECIATED AND GAVE THE FAMILY MUCH COMFORT. Thank you.

OUR FAMILY IS PROUD TO KNOW THAT MY FATHER WAS A MEMBER OF A GROUP OF MEN WHO COLLECTIVELY AND INDIVIDUALLY ARE REPRESENTATIVE OF BLACK MEN WHO CONTINUE TO CONTRIBUTE TO THE YOUTH AND TO THE LARGER COMMUNITY. YOU ARE THE PERSONIFICATION OF STRENGTH IN FELLOWSHIP AND MODEL CITIZENS.

I WISH TO EXPRESS A SPECIAL AND VERY WARM THANK YOU TO ALPHA BROTHER ANTHONY   THURSTON. BROTHER THURSTON, YOUR REMARKS WERE VERY DESCRIPTIVE, ACCURATE AND WELL THOUGHT OUT. YOU CAPTURED THE ESSENCE OF DONALD WHEAT. IN FACT, SEVERAL OF MY CHILDHOOD FRIENDS COMMENTED ABOUT YOUR DELIVERY, YOUR ELEGANCE, AND YOUR UNDERSTANDING OF DONALD WHEAT. THEY INDICATED THAT THEY KNEW MY FATHER AS A FRIEND AND MENTOR FOR HALF A CENTURY AND VERY MUCH WOULD LIKE TO HAVE A COPY OF YOUR REMARKS.

FINALLY, I MUST TELL YOU THAT YOU THAT EACH OF YOU LOOKED KINGLY AND HANDSOME.

DrBatty8@aol.com

Dr. Constance J. Batty

Figure 62 Letter of Appreciation to Alpha Brothers, May 9, 2004

Businesswoman, Cottager, Polar Bear Lived with Zest

Irma L. Wheat, an active citizen of Oak Bluffs and St. Petersburg, Fla., died peacefully on August 9 at the Falmouth Care and Rehabilitation Center in Falmouth. She was 96.

Mrs. Wheat, a daughter of the late James and Lucille Walker, spent her early years in Manhattan, N.Y. She was a businesswoman who, along with her husband, owned and operated a successful luncheonette and stationery store in Corona. The Wheats promoted and sponsored many social events for the community and were responsible for bringing well-known entertainers to the Long Island community.

In the 1950s, the Wheats moved to Roxbury, N.Y., a farming village where they purchased a 150-acre farm. It was in Roxbury that Irma, along with her husband, started and developed a major wholesale butter and egg bonded trucking business. Wheat's Eggs Inc. During these years Wheat's, the only African American bonded egg and butter trucker in New York State, purchased eggs from chicken farmers throughout the Catskill Mountains.

In 1962, the Wheats lost their only son, Donald Jr., age seven, in a tragic auto accident. Irma and Donald went to Europe for a few weeks to gather strength and to regroup. The trip grew into two years of extensive travel around Europe and Africa.

The Wheats returned to the United States but ultimately returned to Europe, purchased a villa in Spain and remained in Europe for seven years. Each year, they returned to the United States to celebrate the Christmas and New Year holidays with their family, and their family sojourned each summer to Spain. Grandchildren attended various camps in Europe while the Wheats and family adults traveled. These were exciting years for Irma Wheat and her family.

During the last 30 years of Mrs. Wheat's life, she lived in Oak Bluffs and St. Petersburg, Fla. She enrolled in a painting class held at the building of the Cottagers, and here she discovered her previously unknown talent. Her paintings were displayed at various art galleries on the Vineyard and were purchased by numerous Vineyard and Florida residents.

Mr. and Mrs. Wheat represented St. Petersburg as delegates to the National Democratic Convention in Chicago when former President William Clinton was nominated. They were active members of the Democratic Party and served on various committees. Mrs. Wheat was

Irma L. Wheat

an active member of the Lakeview Presbyterian Church in St. Petersburg.

While in Oak Bluffs, she was an avid bridge player and a charter member of the Martha's Vineyard chapter of a national bridge association. She was a member of the Polar Bears group and served as a leader of the water exercises. For many years she served on various committees of the Cottagers' organization, and until her death she was the oldest member.

Irma Wheat had a real zest for living, enjoyed traveling, the opera, museums, reading, the theatre, entertaining and being entertained. She was noted for her cheery disposition and her radiant smile.

She is survived by her daughter, Dr. Constance J. Batty of St. Petersburg and Oak Bluffs; and two grandchildren, Judith Batty Esq. and Alicia Batts Esq., as well as two great-grandchildren, all of Washington, D.C.; a sister, Ruth W. Miles of Washington and a host of nieces, nephews and friends. She was predeceased by two children, Judith and Donald.

Contributions in her memory may be sent to Lakeview Presbyterian Church or Hospice of Martha's Vineyard, P.O. Box 2549, Oak Bluffs MA 02557.

Correction

A photograph published in the August 13 Gazette of Vernon Jordan at the Union Chapel in Oak Bluffs incorrectly identified the person Mr. Jordan was standing with. It is Union Chapel president Alphonse Carter. The Gazette regrets the error.

Figure 63 Irma Wheat Obituary (Vineyard Vacations, Inc., 2010)

Acknowledgments

The family of the late Irma L. Wheat requests that Memorial gifts may be sent to one of the following:

Lakeview Presbyterian Church
1310 22nd Ave. South
St. Petersburg, Fl 33705

Hospice of Martha's Vineyard
P. O. Box 1549
Oak Bluffs, MA 02557

Council of Aging
Supportive Day Program
P. O. Box 1729
Vineyard Haven, MA 02568

In Loving Memory Of

Irma L. Wheat

Sunrise
March 15, 1914

Sunset
August 9, 2010

Obituary
Irma L. Wheat

Irma Wheat, an active citizen of Oak Bluffs, MA and St. Petersburg, Florida died peacefully on August 9th at the Falmouth Care and Rehabilitation Center, Falmouth, MA, she was 96.

Mrs. Wheat, a daughter of the late James and Lucille Walker spent her early years in Manhattan, New York. Mrs. Wheat was a business woman who, along with her husband, owned and operated a successful Luncheonette and Stationary store in Corona. The Wheats promoted and sponsored many social events for the community and were responsible for bringing well-known entertainers to the Long Island community.

In the 1950's, the Wheats moved to Roxbury, New York, a farming village where they purchased a 150 acre farm. It was in Roxbury that Irma, along with her husband, started and developed a major wholesale butter and egg bonded trucking business, Wheat's Eggs Inc. During these years Wheat's, the only African-Americans bonded egg and butter trucker in New York State, purchased eggs from chicken farmers throughout the Catskill Mountains.

In 1962, the Wheats lost their only son, Donald Jr., seven years of age, in a tragic auto accident. Irma and Donald went to Europe for a few weeks to gather strength and to regroup. This trip grew into two years of extensive travel around Europe and Africa.

The Wheats returned to the United States but ultimately returned to Europe, purchased a villa in Spain and remained in Europe for seven years. Each year, the Wheats returned to the United States to celebrate the Christmas and New Year holidays with their family, and their family sojourned each summer to Spain. Grandchildren attended various camps in Europe while the Wheat's and family adults traveled. These were exciting years for Irma Wheat and her family.

During the last 30 years of Mrs. Wheat's life, she lived in Oak Bluffs and St. Petersburg, Florida. Mrs. Wheat enrolled in a painting class held at the building of the cottagers (an organization of African American Vineyard Homeowners) and here, Mrs. Wheat discovered her previously unknown talent. Her paintings were displayed at various art galleries on the Vineyard and were purchased by numerous Vineyard and Florida Residents.

Mr. and Mrs. Wheat represented St. Petersburg as delegates to the National Democratic Convention in Chicago when former President William Clinton was nominated. They were active member of the Democratic Party and served on various committees. Mrs. Wheat was an active member of the Lakeview Presbyterian Church in St Petersburg.

While in Oak Bluffs, Mrs Wheat was an avid bridge player, and a charter member of the Martha's Vineyard chapter of a national bridge association. Mrs. Wheat was a member of the "Polar Bears" water group and served as a leader of the water exercises. For many years she served on various committees of the Cottager's organization and until her death she was the oldest member.

Irma Wheat had a real zest for living, enjoyed traveling, the opera, museums, reading, the theatre, entertaining and being entertained. She was noted for her cheery disposition and her radiant smile.

Irma Wheat is survived by her daughter, Dr. Constance J. Batty of St. Petersburg and Oak Bluffs, two grandchildren, Judith Batty ESQ. and Alicia Batts ESQ. as well as two great grandchildren all of Washington, DC; a sister-in-law Mrs.Ruth W. Miles of Washington, DC, a brother Kenneth Walker of Chicago, Ill and a host of nieces, nephews and friends. She was predeceased by two children, Judith and Donald Jr. and her husband of 72 years, Donald Wheat.

Order of Service

Welcome:
Dr. Alphose H. Carter
Union Chapel, President

Opening Remarks:
Mr. James Davis
Church Elder & Family Friend

Scriptures:
Constance Teixeira

In Remembrance:
- *Margaret Williams - Family Friend*
- *Thelma Hurd - Bridge Partner*
- *Erin Walker - Niece*
- *Arlene McKeithan - Daughter of Irma's Friend*

Musical Selection:
Michelle Holland, Soloist

Remarks - *Two Minutes Each, Please*

Closing:
Emily Batts - Great Grand Child

Officiated By: Dr. Constance Batty, Daughter

Figure 64 Irma Walker Wheat Service

Bibliography &
Permissions

*Written permission has been granted for all the works listed below
and is available upon request.*

Britannica, T. E. (2018, March 23). Jack Johnson. Retrieved from Britannica: https://www.britannica.com/biography/Jack-Johnson

Melissa. (2014, January 2014). What Was Life Like In 1914? Retrieved from "Termite" Terry Pest Control Blog: https://termiteterry.com/life-like-1914/

Nelson, J. (2005). Constance Batty. In J. Nelson, Finding Martha's Vineyard (pp. 165-166). Double Day.

New Orleans, L. M.-1. (n.d.). Retrieved from Ancestry.com: Ancestry.com

Tye, L. (2005). Rising from The Rails: Pullman Porters and the Making of the Black Middle Class. New York: Henry Holt and Co.

Vineyard Vacations, Inc. (2004). Donald Wheat, 89, Was Businessman and Mentor. Vineyard Gazette/MV Magazine.

Vineyard Vacations, Inc. (2004, September 16). No Title. Vineyard Gazette/MV Magazine, p. Cover.

Vineyard Vacations, Inc. (2010, August 17). Businesswoman, Cottager, Polar Bear Lived with Zest. Vineyard Gazette/MV Magazine.

About the Author

Constance Wheat Batty B.S., M.A., Ed.D. is a retired educator who served as a faculty member and senior administrator in the State University of New York (SUNY). She was selected as the 2014 SUNY at Fredonia outstanding alumna. She resides at Point Brittany in St. Petersburg, Florida, at Oak Bluffs, on Martha's Vineyard, and sometimes in Washington DC. Dr. Batty has traveled worldwide with both her parents and children. She is a writer of professional literature, a lecturer, a speaker and a participant in many community organizations. She has two daughters, both successful lawyers, and enjoys her grandchildren.

9/17/76
Dubrovnik, Yugoslavia -

Dear Connie & Bean,

We are fine. We just bought the Herald Trib and read about the earthquakes in Italy, Yugoslavia. It did not come near us. We are way in the southern part. That happened in the northern section. Daddy said I knew they must be worried hence this letter. I have already sent 2 cards to Alicia & Judy. Hope they get them soon. The weather here is very warm. In fact practically all the time we have been traveling it has been nice and warm.

Yesterday we took a cruise out on the Adriatic to a little island where they served us some very good home made cheese and wine. Afterwards we had delicious grilled fish and salad. Many people went swimming but it was a mite to cool for us. Met some people who lived in Batavia and had worked at Grassingers so they also knew where Roxbury was. Small world eh?

This morning we visited the old walled in city of Dubrovnik. It's not hard to imagine what it was like in Medieval times. You enter by a draw bridge and Viola! you are back in the 14 & 15th century. The old city's main st. is surprisingly very wide. It was planned by architects and its not a labyrinth but a well planned city completely walled in. One can walk around the ramparts and the walls. It is very well preserved. Some buildings date back as far as the year 1290. Europe first orphanage was here circa 1432. Daddy and I enjoyed strolling around amid hordes literally hundreds

118

of people (most yugoslavians) evidently their special
pleasure is strolling in the evening. We stopped at a
small, clean restaurant run by three young women. The
food real yugoslavian was excellent! Took a bus back
to our hotel to get ready for our trip to Skopje
tomorrow. It most likely will take (2) days. From
there we hope to get a train to take us to Istanbul.
Will write you there.

I sent a card to Mrs Gillespie & Mrs Wylie
Joan Stukie's mother. Hope she is better. I was going to
tell you to write us in care of Hotel Hilton,
Istanbul, but Daddy said it would not give
you enough notice. Wish I had thought of
it sooner. Would love to hear from all of you.
However you can still write to Spain. When
we arrive there it would be very nice to get
a letter from home.

Oh our diet is shot! The bread and butter here is delicious we
just can't stop eating it. I just had a hot cup of tea in
our room with some bread and butter as a night cap.
Ho Hum must diet like crazy when we get back to
Spain. So long must get some sleep. Will write
soon. Love to all

Mother & Daddy.

P.S. Anyway we should be in Istanbul
by the 21st of Sept—

P.SS. DON'T FORGET TO PUT MONEY IN BANK. WE PAID TAXES &
AIRPLANE TICKETS FOR Alicia & Pam. NOT MUCH IN THERE NOW.
M.